D1438392

STUDY THROUGH
THE AGES

STUDY THROUGH THE AGES

Robert Wyeth

Copyright © 2017 by Robert Wyeth.

Library of Congress Control Number: 2017915375
ISBN: Hardcover   978-1-5434-8714-5
               Softcover   978-1-5434-8713-8
               eBook   978-1-5434-8712-1

All rights reserved. No part of this book may be reproduced or transmitted in any form or by any means, electronic or mechanical, including photocopying, recording, or by any information storage and retrieval system, without permission in writing from the copyright owner.

Any people depicted in stock imagery provided by Thinkstock are models, and such images are being used for illustrative purposes only.
Certain stock imagery © Thinkstock.

Print information available on the last page.

Rev. date: 10/18/2017

To order additional copies of this book, contact:
Xlibris
1-888-795-4274
www.Xlibris.com
Orders@Xlibris.com
763133

Contents

Section 3
*No Differences between the Old
Testament and New Testament*

Age	153
Almighty	155
Amen	157
Ambassador	159
Angel	161
Antichrist	164
Apostle	166
Ashes	168
Assurance	171
Atonement	173
Authority	175
Banner	177
Banquet	179
Baptism	181
Beard	183
Beast	185
Birthday	187
Blasphemy	189
Body	191
Bones	194
Branch	197
Brook	199
Captain	201
Cave	203
Chariot	205
Christian	207
Church	209
Compassion	211
Conscience	213
Corruption	215
Council	217
Crime	219
Dance	221
Debt	223
Deceit	225
Demon	227
Devil	229
Disciple	231
Disease	233
Dream	235
Earnest	237
Eden	239
Elder	241
Exile	243
Firstborn	245
Fish	247
Flesh	250
Flood	253
Foot	256
Garden	259
Generation	261
Gentleness	263
Giant	265
Glass	267
Godliness	269
Gospel	271
Government	273
Governor	275
Guest	277
Hair	279
Hail	282
Hate	284
Health	287
Hell	289
Hire	291
Holiness	293
Hook	295
Horn	297
Horse	300
Hospitality	302

Subject Matter

It doesn't really matter when the books were written or published. Even so, it would be helpful to lay out exactly when the text was produced. Genesis would come before Exodus. The dates of the kings can help when the books were produced. Isaiah comes before Jeremiah because the Assyrian Empire came before the Babylonian Empire, and the New Testament comes after the Old Testament.

It is not an exact science, but it makes it easier to understand. I have given you a chronological outline, but several books were unknown, because they do not contain anything that makes them dateable, so I have suggested a possible date.

For example, look at the discipline in the early church.

In AD 61, Paul wrote to his friend Philemon not to apply the letter of the law and have his slave Onesimos executed for theft and desertion. (Philemon ch.1)

In AD 63, apparently as a direct result of lying to God, Ananias and Sapphira died, leaving bystanders in a state of shock. (Acts ch.5)

Later in AD 64, Paul said not to engage in blame unless it is brought by more than one witness. Those who are to be rebuked publicly, so that other men may take warning. (1 Timothy ch.5)

As the years progressed, the people were moved to accept those who find it hard to welcome the discipline of the early church. It gradually changed in the New Testament from death to being reprimanded.

The Inspiration of the Bible

I believe that the Bible was written as a whole, not a lot of separate books. God was in control, and he made sure that when the authors of the books were minded to write things down, he masterminded the sovereignty that came to us. It was not a lot of individual writings.

Take, for example, 'vision'.

There many cases of 'vision', like sight, perception, discernment, foresight, picture, image, dream, illusion, ghost. But God, in his wisdom, decided that the Bible authors should make 'vision' where God speaks during the night.

For over one thousand, seven hundred years, each time a book was published, it was the same thing, God directed it The authors couldn't have known what the others said. The books were not written down in a distinct form; they were localised bodies of writing.

All the books of the Bible maintain that God was the influence, and he decided over the many years that what we can read today, which means that God has foresight and authority. He had a message for us, and nowhere in the Bible is that stated or referenced. It was a collection of books, covering the whole of one's life. It was a 'Manual of Christian Living'.

What I have done is to draw your attention to where in the Old Testament and New Testament are very different, or the same. I will let you draw your own opinions, your own study from the Bible.

The Chronological Bible

(when the books were written or published)

Genesis	1680 BC
Exodus	1280 BC
Leviticus, Numbers and Deuteronomy	1240 BC
Joshua	1220 BC
Ruth	1150 BC
Judges	1060 BC
1 Samuel	1010 BC
2 Samuel and 1 Chronicles	975 BC
1 Kings	850 BC
2 Kings and 2 Chronicles	580 BC
Esther	465 BC
Ezra	450 BC
Nehemiah	400 BC

Amos and Jonah	750 BC
Hosea	720 BC
Micah	690 BC
Isaiah	685 BC
Nahum	630 BC
Zephaniah	625 BC
Habakkuk	620 BC
Jeremiah and Lamentations	580 BC
Obadiah and Ezekiel	570 BC
Joel	550 BC unknown?
Daniel	530 BC
Haggai and Zechariah	515 BC
Malachi	445 BC

Job	1300 BC unknown?
Psalms	1000 BC unknown?
Proverbs, Song of Songs and Ecclesiastes	950 BC unknown?

Matthew, Mark, Luke and John	AD 30
1 Thessalonians	AD 49
2 Thessalonians	AD 50
1 Corinthians and Philippians	AD 53
Galatians	AD 54 unknown?
2 Corinthians and Romans	AD 55
Ephesians, Colossians and Philemon	AD 61
Acts	AD 63
1 and 2 Timothy, Titus and 1 Peter	AD 64
Hebrews and James	AD 66
2 Peter and Jude	AD 80 unknown?
1, 2 and 3 John	AD 93
Revelation	AD 96

A Summary of the Book

Most Popular Old and New Testament

Which book contains the most verses, and why is that important?
What difference would it make if another book contained additional,
or more verses? Why is that significant? What difference would it
make if one book was omitted, like Ecclesiastes or Acts?

And this is what I have done to make it easier to read:

Pentateuch	Gospels
Joshua and Judges	Acts
History books	Letters of Paul
After captivity	Letter of James
Psalms	Letters of Peter
Proverbs and Ecclesiastes	Pastoral Epistles
Major prophets	Hebrews
Minor prophets	Revelation

The Old Testament

The *Pentateuch* (from Genesis to Deuteronomy) contains the history
of the world up until the Israelites go across the river Jordan to
conquer the Promised Land.

Joshua and Judges contain the Promised Land up until they decide to
go for a king.

History books incorporate King Saul up until the exile.

After captivity takes into account from the exile up until the Old
Testament finishes.

Psalms, Proverbs and Ecclesiastes take into account the wisdom
books.

Major Prophets include Isaiah, Jeremiah and Ezekiel, which will have the most material.

Minor Prophets include Daniel to Malachi.

The New Testament

The *Gospels* contain Matthew, Mark, Luke and John, regarding the life of Jesus.

Acts comes after Jesus was glorified, up until Paul was murdered.

The *Letters of Paul* (from Romans to Philemon) deal with the situation and problems of the churches.

This *Letter of James* to the Jewish Christians.

The *Letters of Peter* are about dealing with persecution outside and false teachers inside the church.

The *Pastoral Epistles* (both Timothy and Titus) Paul wrote these in his later life, in prison.

Hebrews contains the temptation to revert back to Judaism.

Revelation is about the final showdown between God and Satan.

A number of books are not included, like Ruth, Job, Lamentations and John's letters. If you have an opinion about them, you can add them to the list.

And I have produced a list of verses (not every verse) to show you how the books develop from start to finish, from 1680 BC to AD 96. To make clear the message I have given you in the meaning. If you don't agree with the meaning, what would you suggest?

Missing and Added Books

So I have added a section to remind you, like the missing and added books. For example, like Jeremiah and Ezekiel but not the prophet Isaiah. Why does it matter? What difference does it make? If one book is absent?

It is really important to study the missing or added books, this is what examining or researching the Bible tells us. What difference would it make if the Pentateuch was missing or Hebrews was added to the list? I think it would be better to make some notes about how the Bible was structured, and then you will be able to understand.

What Meaning Is There in the Old and New Testaments?

Rather than go through the text, looking through the verses, I will give you a brief explanation. You might have another opinion; that's why we study the Bible. I have tried to be brief and not to overshadow you with words. For in Section 1, you will have two options one for the Old Testament and one for the New Testament. But in Section 3, you will only have one option for the Bible.

How Many Verses Are There in the Old and New Testaments?

I have used the New Living Translation (NLT) in this book, but you might use another version of the Bible. If you are clever, you can do the 'Hebrew Bible' and the 'Greek Testament Versions', but you might have problems reconciling the text. Like, 'child' there are three references in the Greek and four words for 'watch' in the Hebrew text.

I have recorded the number of verses found. I have tended to seek only a few verses; otherwise, you may not notice the differences in the Bible. So I have ignored place names and individual names. You could always add your study to mine. The purpose is to really read the Bible, it doesn't matter if there is a difference between your work and mine. So examine and study the Bible!

Section 1

Differences between the Old Testament and New Testament

Adultery

Most popular Old Testament Jeremiah and Ezekiel.	Most popular New Testament Matthew.
If the book is missing, it would be **bold** Pentateuch **Joshua and Judges** **History books** After captivity Psalms Proverbs and Ecclesiastes Major prophets Minor prophets	Gospels **Acts** Letters of Paul Letter of James Letters of Peter **Pastoral Epistles** Hebrews Revelation
Missing books Why is it not in the History Books?	
Added books Why is it in Matthew's Gospel?	
What meaning is there in the Old Testament If you commit adultery, you will be put to death.	What meaning is there in the New Testament Remain faithful to each other in marriage.
How many verses in the Old Testament Thirty-six.	How many verses in the New Testament Thirty-three.

1280 BC
Exodus ch.20 v14

1240 BC
Leviticus ch.20 v10
Deuteronomy ch.5 v18; ch.22 v22

1000 BC
Psalm ch.106 v39

950 BC
Proverbs ch.6 v32

720 BC
Hosea ch.4 v14

685 BC
Isaiah ch.57 v7

580 BC
Jeremiah ch.3 v8-10

570 BC
Ezekiel ch.22 v11-12

AD 30
Matthew ch.5 v27-29, v32
Mark ch.10 v11-12
John ch.8 4-11

AD 55
Romans ch.7 v3

AD 66
Hebrews ch.13 v4

AD 80
2 Peter ch.2 v14

AD 96
Revelation ch.2 v22

Blessing

Most popular Old Testament	Most popular New Testament
Genesis.	Luke and Hebrews.
If the book is missing, it would be **bold**	Gospels
Pentateuch	Acts
Joshua and Judges	Letters of Paul
History books	Letter of James
After captivity	Letters of Peter
Psalms	**Pastoral Epistles**
Proverbs and Ecclesiastes	Hebrews
Major prophets	Revelation
Minor prophets	

Missing books

Why is it not in the Pastoral Epistles?

Added books

Why is it in Luke's Gospel?

What meaning is there in the Old Testament	What meaning is there in the New Testament
Famous people give their blessing to others.	God's blessing would be to carry on as we are doing.
How many verses in the Old Testament	How many verses in the New Testament
Seventy-two.	Twenty-nine.

1680 BC
Genesis ch.12 v2-3; ch.14 v19-20; ch.27 v33-35

1280 BC
Exodus ch.32 v29

1240 BC
Leviticus ch.25 v21-22
Deuteronomy ch.11 v26-28; ch.28 v8

1000 BC
Psalm ch.37 v26

975 BC
2 Samuel ch.7 v29

950 BC
Proverbs ch.5 v18

685 BC
Isaiah ch.65 v16

580 BC
2 Chronicles ch.20 v26

570 BC
Ezekiel ch.34 v26-27

400 BC
Nehemiah ch.9 v5-6

515 BC
Zechariah ch.8 v13

445 BC
Malachi ch.3 v10-11

AD 30
Matthew ch.10 v12-14
Luke ch.14 v15; ch.24 v51-53

AD 53
1 Corinthians ch.16 v11

AD 54
Galatians ch.6 v9-10

AD 55
Romans ch.11 v12
2 Corinthians ch.1 v15

AD 61
Ephesians ch.1 v3-4

AD 63
Acts ch.4 v33-34; ch.15 v33-35

AD 64
1 Peter ch.3 v9-10

AD 66
Hebrews ch.6 v7-8

Blood

Most popular Old Testament	Most popular New Testament
Leviticus.	Hebrews.

If the book is missing, it would be **bold**	
	Gospels
Pentateuch	Acts
Joshua and Judges	Letters of Paul
History books	**Letter of James**
After captivity	Letters of Peter
Psalms	**Pastoral Epistles**
Proverbs and Ecclesiastes	Hebrews
Major prophets	Revelation
Minor prophets	

Missing books
Why is it not in Proverbs?

Added books
Why is it in Leviticus?

What meaning is there in the Old Testament	What meaning is there in the New Testament
The only blood that can appease God is that of animals.	God presented Jesus as the sacrifice for sin.

How many verses in the Old Testament	How many verses in the New Testament
Two hundred and Twenty-seven.	Seventy-seven.

1680 BC
Genesis ch.9 v5-7

1280 BC
Exodus ch.12 v7-8; ch.23 v18; ch.24 v8

1240 BC
Leviticus ch.3 v17; ch.7 v2-3; ch.17 v11-12

975 BC
1 Chronicles ch.28 v3

685 BC
Isaiah ch.1 v11

580 BC
2 Kings ch.21 v16
Jeremiah ch.19 v4-5

570 BC
Ezekiel ch.22 v4

AD 30
John ch.6 v53-57

AD 53
1 Corinthians ch.11 v25

AD 55
Romans ch.3 v25

AD 61
Ephesians ch.1 v7-8

AD 63
Acts ch.2 v20

AD 66
Hebrews ch.9 v22

AD 80
1 Peter ch.1 v19-20

AD 96
Revelation ch.7 v14; ch.19 v13-14

Burden

Most popular Old Testament	Most popular New Testament
Isaiah.	2 Corinthians.
If the book is missing, it would be **bold** Pentateuch **Joshua and Judges** History books After captivity Psalms Proverbs and Ecclesiastes Major prophets Minor prophets	Gospels Acts Letters of Paul **Letter of James** **Letters of Peter** **Pastoral Epistles** **Hebrews** **Revelation**
Missing books Why is it not in Genesis?	
Added books Why is it in the two books of Thessalonians?	
What meaning is there in the Old Testament The word burden means suffering.	What meaning is there in the New Testament Preaching the Good News is not a burden.
How many verses in the Old Testament Twenty-two.	How many verses in the New Testament Twelve.

1300 BC
Job ch.7 v20

1280 BC
Exodus ch.2 v23-24; ch.18 v18-19

1240 BC
Numbers ch.11 v11-12

1010 BC
1 Samuel ch.25 v31

1000 BC
Psalm ch.38 v4

950 BC
Ecclesiastes ch.3 v10-11

975 BC
2 Samuel ch.19 v35-36

720 BC
Hosea ch.8 v10

685 BC
Isaiah ch.1 v4; ch.26 v16; ch.58 v6

580 BC
2 Chronicles ch.10 v10-11
Jeremiah ch.23 v33

400 BC
Nehemiah ch.5 v18

AD 30
Matthew ch.11 v30
Luke ch.12 v50-51

AD 49
1 Thessalonians ch.2 v9-10

AD 50
2 Thessalonians ch.3 v8-9

AD 55
2 Corinthians ch.11 v9-10, v28-29; ch.12 v13

AD 63
Acts ch.15 v28-29

Calling

Most popular Old Testament	Most popular New Testament
Isaiah.	Mark and Acts.
If the book is missing, it would be **bold** Pentateuch **Joshua and Judges** History books After captivity Psalms **Proverbs and Ecclesiastes** Major prophets Minor prophets	Gospels Acts Letters of Paul **Letter of James** **Letters of Peter** **Pastoral Epistles** **Hebrews** Revelation
Missing books Why is it not in Ecclesiastes?	
Added books Why is it in Isaiah?	
What meaning is there in the Old Testament Calling indicates a person or persons.	What meaning is there in the New Testament It means you have been called by God.
How many verses in the Old Testament Twenty-two.	How many verses in the New Testament Fifteen.

1240 BC
Numbers ch.10 v2-3

1010 BC
1 Samuel ch.3 v8-9; ch.28 v15

750 BC
Amos ch.4 v1

685 BC
Isaiah ch.6 v3; ch.40 v26

580 BC
Jeremiah ch.1 v15

AD 30
Matthew ch.25 v11-12; ch.27 v37-48
Mark ch.8 v34-35
Luke ch.6 v46-47

AD 53
1 Corinthians ch.6 v11
Philippians ch.3 v14

AD 61
Ephesians ch.4 v1-2

AD 63
Acts ch.9 v10; ch.16 v10; ch.22 v16

AD 93
1 John ch.5 v10

AD 96
Revelation ch.18 v4

Clean

Most popular Old Testament	Most popular New Testament
Leviticus.	Matthew and Luke.

If the book is missing, it would be **bold**	
	Gospels
Pentateuch	Acts
Joshua and Judges	Letters of Paul
History books	**Letter of James**
After captivity	Letters of Peter
Psalms	Pastoral Epistles
Proverbs and Ecclesiastes	Hebrews
Major prophets	**Revelation**
Minor prophets	

Missing books
Why is it not in Revelation?

Added books
Why is it in Ezekiel?

What meaning is there in the Old Testament	What meaning is there in the New Testament
Clean means preparing for God's use.	It means live innocent lives for God.

How many verses in the Old Testament	How many verses in the New Testament
Eighty-four.	Twenty.

1680 BC
Genesis ch.20 v5

1300 BC
Job ch.11 v4

1240 BC
Leviticus ch.6 v10-11; ch.7 v19-20; ch.11 v36-38; ch.13 v6-7, v40-42;
ch.14 v53
Numbers ch.9 v13

1010 BC
1 Samuel ch.12 v5; ch.21 v5

1000 BC
Psalm ch.51 v9-10

950 BC
Ecclesiastes ch.9 v2

685 BC
Isaiah ch.1 v16-17

580 BC
Jeremiah ch.2 v22

570 BC
Ezekiel ch.36 v25-26

AD 30
Mark ch.1 v40
Luke ch.11 v41
John ch.13 v10-11

AD 53
Philippians ch.2 v15-16

AD 63
Acts ch.10 v15-16

AD 61
Ephesians ch.5 v25-26

AD 64
2 Timothy ch.2 v21

AD 66
Hebrews ch.10 v22

Cloud

Most popular Old Testament Exodus.	Most popular New Testament Revelation.
If the book is missing, it would be **bold** Pentateuch Joshua and Judges History books After captivity Psalms Proverbs and Ecclesiastes Major prophets **Minor prophets**	Gospels Acts Letters of Paul **Letter of James** **Letters of Peter** **Pastoral Epistles** **Hebrews** Revelation
Missing books Why is it not in Hebrews?	
Added books Why is it in Numbers?	
What meaning is there in the Old Testament A thick dark cloud is where God reigns.	What meaning is there in the New Testament A cloud is where Jesus lives in glory.
How many verses in the Old Testament Eighty-two.	How many verses in the New Testament Seventeen.

1300 BC
Job ch.3 v5; ch.7 v9-10; ch.30 v15-16

1280 BC
Exodus ch.13 v21-22; ch.16 v10; ch.20 v21; ch.40 v38

1240 BC
Leviticus ch.16 v2
Numbers ch.9 v21-22

1060 BC
Judges ch.20 v38-39

950 BC
Ecclesiastes ch.5 v16-17

850 BC
1 Kings ch.8 v12-13; ch.18 v43-44

685 BC
Isaiah ch.25 v7; ch.44 v22

570 BC
Ezekiel ch.1 v4; ch.32 v7-8; ch.38 v9

AD 30
Matthew ch.17 v5-6
Luke ch.21 v27-28

AD 63
Acts ch.1 v9-11

AD 96
Revelation ch.10 v1-2; ch.11 v12; ch.14 v14-16

Creation

Most popular Old Testament	Most popular New Testament
Genesis.	Romans.
If the book is missing, it would be **bold** Pentateuch **Joshua and Judges** **History books** **After captivity** Psalms **Proverbs and Ecclesiastes** Major prophets Minor prophets	Gospels **Acts** Letters of Paul Letter of James **Letters of Peter** **Pastoral Epistles** Hebrews Revelation
Missing books Why is it not in John's Gospel?	
Added books Why is it in Romans?	
What meaning is there in the Old Testament God created the world and everything in it.	What meaning is there in the New Testament We can share his new creation.
How many verses in the Old Testament Eight.	How many verses in the New Testament Sixteen.

1680 BC
Genesis ch.2 v2-3

1000 BC
Psalm ch.145 v9

685 BC
Isaiah ch.65 v18

620 BC
Habakkuk ch.2 v18

AD 30
Matthew ch.13 v35; ch.25 v34
Mark ch.10 v6-7
Luke ch.11 v50

AD 54
Galatians ch.6 v15-16

AD 55
Romans ch.8 v19-23, v39

AD 61
Colossians ch.1 v15

AD 66
Hebrews ch.4 v13; ch.12 v27
James ch.1 v18

Crown

Most popular Old Testament	Most popular New Testament
Proverbs.	Revelation.

If the book is missing, it would be **bold**	
	Gospels
Pentateuch	**Acts**
Joshua and Judges	Letters of Paul
History books	Letter of James
After captivity	Letters of Peter
Psalms	Pastoral Epistles
Proverbs and Ecclesiastes	**Hebrews**
Major prophets	Revelation
Minor prophets	

Missing books
Why is it not in Luke's Gospel?

Added books
Why is it in Zechariah?

What meaning is there in the Old Testament	What meaning is there in the New Testament
A crown is befitting for a king.	Crown involves staying loyal to the faith.

How many verses in the Old Testament	How many verses in the New Testament
Thirty-three.	Fourteen.

1300 BC
Job ch.19 v9

1000 BC
Psalm ch.21 v3; ch.89 v39

975 BC
2 Samuel ch.12 v30

950 BC
Proverbs ch.12 v4; ch.14 v24; ch.16 v31

685 BC
Isaiah ch.28 v3; ch.61 v3; ch.62 v3

580 BC
2 Kings ch.11 v12

515 BC
Zechariah ch.6 v11-12

465 BC
Esther ch.1 v11-12; ch.2 v17-18; ch.8 v15

AD 30
John ch.19 v5

AD 49
1 Thessalonians ch.2 v19-20

AD 53
Philippians ch.4 v1

AD 64
2 Timothy ch.4 v8
1 Peter ch.5 v4

AD 66
James ch.1 v12-13

AD 96
Revelation ch.2 v10; ch.3 v11; ch.6 v2; ch.12 v1-2

Curse

Most popular Old Testament Numbers.	Most popular New Testament Galatians.
If the book is missing, it would be **bold** Pentateuch Joshua and Judges History books After captivity Psalms Proverbs and Ecclesiastes Major prophets Minor prophets	Gospels Acts Letters of Paul **Letter of James** Letters of Peter **Pastoral Epistles** **Hebrews** Revelation
Missing books Why is it not in Ezekiel?	
Added books Why is it in Galatians?	
What meaning is there in the Old Testament Something awful is going to happen to you.	What meaning is there in the New Testament Speak kindly to those who curse you.
How many verses in the Old Testament Eighty-nine.	How many verses in the New Testament Seventeen.

1680 BC
Genesis ch.8 v21-22; ch.12 v3; ch.27 v12

1300 BC
Job ch.2 v5; ch.3 v10

1280 BC
Exodus ch.22 v11

1240 BC
Leviticus ch.24 v14-16
Numbers ch.5 v24; ch.22 v11
Deuteronomy ch.11 v26-28

1060 BC
Judges ch.17 v2

1010 BC
1 Samuel ch.14 v24-25

1000 BC
Psalm ch.10 v3

950 BC
Proverbs ch.11 v26

685 BC
Isaiah ch.8 v21-22; ch.24 v6

580 BC
Jeremiah ch.23 v10

445 BC
Malachi ch.3 v8-10

AD 30
Matthew ch.5 v22

Mark ch.14 v71-72
Luke ch.6 v28-29

AD 54
Galatians ch.1 v8-9; ch.3 v13

AD 55
Romans ch.12 v14-15

AD 80
2 Peter ch.2 v14-15

Desire

Most popular Old Testament	Most popular New Testament
Psalms.	1 Corinthians and 2 Peter.

If the book is missing, it would be **bold**	
	Gospels
Pentateuch	Acts
Joshua and Judges	Letters of Paul
History books	Letter of James
After captivity	Letters of Peter
Psalms	Pastoral Epistles
Proverbs and Ecclesiastes	Hebrews
Major prophets	**Revelation**
Minor prophets	

Missing books
Why is it not in Revelation?

Added books
Why is it in Luke's Gospel?

What meaning is there in the Old Testament	What meaning is there in the New Testament
Desire is where God would honour his people.	Desire means that God is working through you.

How many verses in the Old Testament	How many verses in the New Testament
Twenty-eight.	Ten.

1680 BC
Genesis ch.3 v16

1300 BC
Job ch.6 v8

1010 BC
1 Samuel ch.2 v35-36

1000 BC
Psalm ch.5 v9; ch.51 v6, v16-17; ch.73 v25; ch.119 v20

975 BC
1 Chronicles ch.28 v2

950 BC
Proverbs ch.21 v10; ch.24 v1; ch.27 v20
Ecclesiastes ch.2 v8; ch.12 v5

685 BC
Isaiah ch.26 v8

580 BC
2 Chronicles ch.1 v11
Jeremiah ch.2 v24; ch.32 v40-41

AD 30
Mark ch.4 v19

AD 63
Acts ch.28 v19-20

AD 53
1 Corinthians ch.12 v31; ch.14 v1-2
Philippians ch.2 v13

AD 64
1 Timothy ch.6 v4-5

AD 66
Hebrews ch.6 v11-12
James ch.5 v5-6

AD 80
2 Peter ch.2 v10, v14

Divorce

Most popular Old Testament Deuteronomy.	Most popular New Testament Matthew.
If the book is missing, it would be **bold** Pentateuch **Joshua and Judges** **History books** After captivity **Psalms** **Proverbs and Ecclesiastes** **Major prophets** Minor prophets	Gospels **Acts** **Letters of Paul** **Letter of James** **Letters of Peter** **Pastoral Epistles** **Hebrews** **Revelation**
Missing books Why is it not in the Major Prophets?	
Added books Why is it in Ezra?	
What meaning is there in the Old Testament Moses allowed a person to divorce his wife.	What meaning is there in the New Testament A man can divorce his wife if she is unfaithful.
How many verses in the Old Testament Seven.	How many verses in the New Testament Eleven.

1240 BC
Deuteronomy ch.22 v19, v39; ch.24 v1-2

450 BC
Ezra ch.10 v2-4, v19

445 BC
Malachi ch.2 v16

AD 30
Matthew ch.5 v31-32; ch.19 v3, v7-9
Mark ch.10 v2-4

Famine

Most popular Old Testament	Most popular New Testament
Jeremiah.	Luke, Acts and Revelation.

If the book is missing, it would be **bold**	
Pentateuch	Gospels
Joshua and Judges	Acts
History books	**Letters of Paul**
After captivity	**Letter of James**
Psalms	**Letters of Peter**
Proverbs and Ecclesiastes	**Pastoral Epistles**
Major prophets	**Hebrews**
Minor prophets	Revelation

Missing books
Why is it not in Proverbs and Ecclesiastes?

Added books
Why is it in Jeremiah?

What meaning is there in the Old Testament	What meaning is there in the New Testament
God would send famine over the land.	A great famine swept over the people.

How many verses in the Old Testament	How many verses in the New Testament
Ninety-four.	Six.

1680 BC
Genesis ch.12 v10-11; ch.41 v36; ch.47 v13-14

1300 BC
Job ch.5 v20

1240 BC
Deuteronomy ch.32 v24

1150 BC
Ruth ch.1 v1

1000 BC
Psalm ch.33 v19; ch.105 v16

975 BC
2 Samuel ch.21 v1

850 BC
1 Kings ch.8 v37-39; ch.18 v2-3

685 BC
Isaiah ch.14 v30; ch.51 v19

580 BC
2 Kings ch.4 v38; ch.25 v3-4
Jeremiah ch.14 v11-12; ch.16 v4
Lamentations ch.5 v10

570 BC
Ezekiel ch.5 v12-13, v17

750 BC
Amos ch.4 v6; ch.8 v11

400 BC
Nehemiah ch.5 v3

AD 30
Luke ch.15 v14

AD 63
Acts ch.11 v28

AD 96
Revelation ch.6 v8

Fasting

Most popular Old Testament Isaiah.	Most popular New Testament Matthew.
If the book is missing, it would be **bold** **Pentateuch** **Joshua and Judges** History books After captivity Psalms **Proverbs and Ecclesiastes** Major prophets Minor prophets	Gospels Acts **Letters of Paul** **Letter of James** **Letters of Peter** **Pastoral Epistles** Hebrews **Revelation**
Missing books Why is it not in Ezekiel?	
Added books Why is it in Joel?	
What meaning is there in the Old Testament They fasted because they wanted the Lord to act.	What meaning is there in the New Testament The people of God relied on fasting and prayer.
How many verses in the Old Testament Nineteen.	How many verses in the New Testament Eleven.

1000 BC
Psalm ch.35 v13; ch.109 v24-25

850 BC
1 Kings ch.21 v9-10

685 BC
Isaiah ch.1 v13-14; ch.58 v3-4

580 BC
2 Chronicles ch.20 v3-4
Jeremiah ch.36 v6

550 BC
Joel ch.1 v14; ch.2 v12-13, v15

530 BC
Daniel ch.6 v18; ch.9 v3

515 BC
Zechariah ch.7 v5-7

465 BC
Esther ch.9 v31-32

AD 30
Matthew ch.6 v16-18
Mark ch.2 v18
Luke ch.2 v37-38

AD 63
Acts ch.13 v2-3; ch.14 v23-24

Forest

Most popular Old Testament	Most popular New Testament
Isaiah.	James.

If the book is missing, it would be **bold**	
Pentateuch	**Gospels**
Joshua and Judges	**Acts**
History books	**Letters of Paul**
After captivity	Letter of James
Psalms	**Letters of Peter**
Proverbs and Ecclesiastes	**Pastoral Epistles**
Major prophets	**Hebrews**
Minor prophets	**Revelation**

Missing books
Why is it not in Ecclesiastes?

Added books
Why is it in the Letter of James

What meaning is there in the Old Testament	What meaning is there in the New Testament
Forest is the place where trees grow close together.	The forest is on fire.

How many verses in the Old Testament	How many verses in the New Testament
Thirty-two.	One.

1240 BC
Deuteronomy ch.19 v5

1220 BC
Joshua ch.17 v15

1010 BC
1 Samuel ch.14 v24-26; ch.22 v5

1000 BC
Psalm ch.50 v10; ch.80 v13; ch.83 v14-15; ch.96 v12; ch.104 v20

975 BC
2 Samuel ch.18 v8, v17
1 Chronicles ch.16 v33

850 BC
1 Kings ch.7 v2

690 BC
Micah ch.5 v8

685 BC
Isaiah ch.10 v18-19; ch.14 v8; ch.32 v19; ch.44 v14

580 BC
Jeremiah ch.5 v6; ch.12 v8

570 BC
Ezekiel ch.15 v6-7

400 BC
Nehemiah ch.2 v8

AD 66
James ch.3 v5-6

Forgiveness

Most popular Old Testament Psalms.	Most popular New Testament Luke.
If the book is missing, it would be **bold** Pentateuch **Joshua and Judges** History books After captivity Psalms **Proverbs and Ecclesiastes** Major prophets **Minor prophets**	Gospels Acts Letters of Paul Letter of James **Letters of Peter** **Pastoral Epistles** Hebrews **Revelation**
Missing books Why is not it in Isaiah and Ezekiel?	
Added books Why is it in Luke's Gospel?	
What meaning is there in the Old Testament Forgiveness means the shedding of blood.	What meaning is there in the New Testament Jesus will offer you forgiveness for your sins.
How many verses in the Old Testament Six.	How many verses in the New Testament Fourteen.

1280 BC
Exodus ch.32 v30

1000 BC
Psalm ch.51 v14; ch.130 v4

580 BC
Jeremiah ch.36 v7

400 BC
Nehemiah ch.9 v17-18

AD 30
Mark ch.1 v4-5
Luke ch.1 v77; ch.17 v3-4; ch.24 v47-48

AD 55
Romans ch.5 v15-16

AD 63
Acts ch.2 v38; ch.13 v38-40; ch.26 v18

AD 66
Hebrews ch.9 v22; ch.12 v24
James ch.5 v20

Foundation

Most popular Old Testament	Most popular New Testament
Psalms.	Luke and 1 Corinthians.
If the book is missing, it would be **bold** **Pentateuch** Joshua and Judges History books After captivity Psalms Proverbs and Ecclesiastes Major prophets Minor prophets	Gospels **Acts** Letters of Paul **Letter of James** Letters of Peter Pastoral Epistles Hebrews Revelation
Missing books Why is it not in the Pentateuch?	
Added books Why is it in Luke's Gospel?	
What meaning is there in the Old Testament God is the foundation for life.	What meaning is there in the New Testament The foundation for the church is Jesus Christ.
How many verses in the Old Testament Thirty-one.	How many verses in the New Testament Seventeen.

1220 BC
Joshua ch.6 v26

1000 BC
Psalm ch.24 v2; ch.89 v14; ch.97 v2; ch.102 v25; ch.111 v10

950 BC
Proverbs ch.1 v7

850 BC
1 Kings ch.5 v17-18; ch.6 v37-38; ch.7 v10-12

750 BC
Amos ch.9 v1, v6

690 BC
Micah ch.3 v10

685 BC
Isaiah ch.33 v6

580 BC
2 Chronicles ch.3 v3-4; ch.23 v5

570 BC
Ezekiel ch.13 v14

515 BC
Zechariah ch.8 v9-10

450 BC
Ezra ch.3 v6, v11

AD 30
Luke ch.6 v48; ch.14 v29-30

AD 53
1 Corinthians ch.3 v10-11

AD 61
Ephesians ch.2 v20-21

AD 64
1 Timothy ch.3 v15; ch.6 v19
2 Timothy ch.2 v19

AD 66
Hebrews ch.1 v10

AD 96
Revelation ch.21 v9

Fruit

Most popular Old Testament Genesis.	Most popular New Testament Matthew.
If the book is missing, it would be **bold** Pentateuch Joshua and Judges History books After captivity Psalms Proverbs and Ecclesiastes Major prophets Minor prophets	Gospels **Acts** Letters of Paul **Letter of James** **Letters of Peter** Pastoral Epistles **Hebrews** Revelation
Missing books Why is it not in Acts?	
Added books Why is it in Genesis?	
What meaning is there in the Old Testament Fruit is something produced by God for the nations.	What meaning is there in the New Testament The fruit is like spiritual fruit.
How many verses in the Old Testament Ninety-eight.	How many verses in the New Testament Forty-two.

1680 BC
Genesis ch.1 v11, v29-30; ch.2 v16-17

1300 BC
Job ch.15 v33

1280 BC
Exodus ch.10 v15

1240 BC
Leviticus ch.19 v23
Numbers ch.13 v26-27
Deuteronomy ch.20 v6-7

1000 BC
Psalm ch.92 v14-15

975 BC
2 Samuel ch.16 v2

950 BC
Proverbs ch.1 v31
Ecclesiastes ch.2 v5-6

750 BC
Amos ch.2 v9-10

720 BC
Hosea ch.2 v12

690 BC
Micah ch.7 v1

685 BC
Isaiah ch.4 v2

580 BC
Jeremiah ch.6 v15

570 BC
Ezekiel ch.17 v9; ch.36 v8-9

550 BC
Joel ch.1 v12-13

515 BC
Zechariah ch.8 v12

400 BC
Nehemiah ch.9 v25

AD 30
Matthew ch.3 v10; ch.7 v16-20
John ch.15 v4

AD 53
Philippians ch.1 v11

AD 54
Galatians ch.5 v22-23

AD 55
Romans ch.1 v13-14

AD 64
2 Timothy ch.2 v6-7

AD 96
Revelation ch.2 v7

Furnace

Most popular Old Testament	Most popular New Testament
Daniel.	Matthew and Revelation.

If the book is missing, it would be **bold**	
	Gospels
Pentateuch	**Acts**
Joshua and Judges	**Letters of Paul**
History books	**Letter of James**
After captivity	**Letters of Peter**
Psalms	**Pastoral Epistles**
Proverbs and Ecclesiastes	**Hebrews**
Major prophets	Revelation
Minor prophets	

Missing books	
Why is it not in Isaiah?	

Added books	
Why is it in Daniel?	

What meaning is there in the Old Testament	What meaning is there in the New Testament
God's people were refined as a furnace.	The Day of Judgement is coming like a furnace.

How many verses in the Old Testament	How many verses in the New Testament
Twenty.	Four.

1680 BC
Genesis ch.19 v28

1240 BC
Deuteronomy ch.4 v20

1000 BC
Psalm ch.12 v6; ch.21 v9

685 BC
Isaiah ch.48 v10

580 BC
Jeremiah ch.11 v4-5

570 BC
Ezekiel ch.22 v20-22

530 BC
Daniel ch.3 v6

445 BC
Malachi ch.4 v1

AD 30
Matthew ch.13 v42-43

AD 96
Revelation ch.1 v15-16; ch.9 v2

Gift

Most popular Old Testament	Most popular New Testament
Leviticus.	Romans and 1 Corinthians.

If the book is missing, it would be **bold**	
	Gospels
Pentateuch	Acts
Joshua and Judges	Letters of Paul
History books	**Letter of James**
After captivity	Letters of Peter
Psalms	Pastoral Epistles
Proverbs and Ecclesiastes	**Hebrews**
Major prophets	**Revelation**
Minor prophets	

Missing books Why is it not in Jeremiah?

Added books Why is it in Leviticus?

What meaning is there in the Old Testament	What meaning is there in the New Testament
There is a gift from the Lord.	The Holy Spirit distributes the gifts.

How many verses in the Old Testament	How many verses in the New Testament
Ninety-four.	Fifty-seven.

1680 BC
Genesis ch.4 v4-5; ch.33 v8; ch.37 v3-4

1280 BC
Exodus ch.16 v29; ch.29 v18

1240 BC
Leviticus ch.2 v16; ch.7 v29-30; ch.27 v9-10
Numbers ch.15 v25-26
Deuteronomy ch.16 v6-7

1220 BC
Joshua ch.15 v19

1010 BC
1 Samuel ch.6 v3

1000 BC
Psalm ch.127 v3

975 BC
2 Samuel ch.11 v8-9

950 BC
Proverbs ch.18 v16; ch.21 v14
Ecclesiastes ch.5 v19-20

850 BC
1 Kings ch.9 v16-17

580 BC
2 Kings ch.8 v8
2 Chronicles ch.9 v9

570 BC
Ezekiel ch.46 v16-17

515 BC
Zechariah ch.13 v4-5

AD 30
Matthew ch.23 v19-20
Luke ch.6 v38
John ch.14 v27

AD 53
1 Corinthians ch.7 v7; ch.12 v7-8, v11

AD 55
Romans ch.4 v16; ch.5 v16-17; ch.6 v23; ch.12 v8
2 Corinthians ch.8 v4-5; ch.9 v15

AD 61
Ephesians ch.4 v7-8

AD 63
Acts ch.1 v4-5; ch.11 v17; ch.21 v9

AD 64
1 Timothy ch.4 v14-15
2 Timothy ch.1 v6-7
1 Peter ch.4 v10-11

Grace

Most popular Old Testament	Most popular New Testament
Deuteronomy, Ezra, Psalms, Proverbs, Isaiah and Zechariah.	Romans.
If the book is missing, it would be **bold** Pentateuch **Joshua and Judges** **History books** After captivity Psalms Proverbs and Ecclesiastes Major prophets Minor prophets	**Gospels** Acts Letters of Paul Letter of James Letters of Peter Pastoral Epistles Hebrews Revelation
Missing books Why is it not in the Gospels?	
Added books Why is it in Romans?	
What meaning is there in the Old Testament The Lord gives us grace.	What meaning is there in the New Testament Grace, mercy and peace are from the Saviour who loves us.
How many verses in the Old Testament Six.	How many verses in the New Testament Eighty-three.

1000 BC
Psalm ch.84 v11

950 BC
Proverbs ch.1 v9

685 BC
Isaiah ch.60 v10

515 BC
Zechariah ch.12 v10

450 BC
Ezra ch.9 v8

AD 63
Acts ch.9 v8-9; ch.14 v3, v26-27; ch.15 v11; ch.18 v27-28; ch.20 v24, v32

AD 50
2 Thessalonians ch.2 v16-17

AD 54
Galatians ch.1 v15

AD 55
Romans ch.5 v15-17; ch.6 v15-16; ch.11 v5-6; ch.12 v6
2 Corinthians ch.1 v12; ch.12 v9

AD 61
Ephesians ch.1 v7-8; ch.3 v2-3
Colossians ch.1 v6

AD 64
1 Timothy ch.1 v2
2 Timothy ch.2 v1-2
Titus ch.2 v11-12

1 Peter ch.5 v12

AD 66
Hebrews ch.4 v16; ch.13 v9
James ch.4 v6

AD 80
Jude ch.1 v4

AD 93
2 John ch.1 v3

Grass

Most popular Old Testament	Most popular New Testament
Isaiah.	1 Peter and Revelation.
If the book is missing, it would be **bold** Pentateuch **Joshua and Judges** History books After captivity Psalms Proverbs and Ecclesiastes Major prophets Minor prophets	Gospels **Acts** **Letters of Paul** Letter of James Letters of Peter **Pastoral Epistles** **Hebrews** Revelation
Missing books Why is it not in the Letters of Paul?	
Added books Why is it in Job?	
What meaning is there in the Old Testament Grass is the product of the fields.	What meaning is there in the New Testament Green grass will wither and die.
How many verses in the Old Testament Fifty-two.	How many verses in the New Testament Seven.

1300 BC
Job ch.5 v25; ch.38 v27

1240 BC
Numbers ch.22 v4
Deuteronomy ch.29 v23; ch.32 v2

1000 BC
Psalm ch.37 v2; ch.72 v16; ch.103 v15

975 BC
2 Samuel ch.23 v4

690 BC
Micah ch.5 v7

685 BC
Isaiah ch.5 v24; ch.37 v27; ch.40 v8

580 BC
2 Kings ch.19 v26
Jeremiah ch.14 v6

530 BC
Daniel ch.4 v33

AD 30
Matthew ch.14 v19

AD 64
1 Peter ch.1 v24-25

AD 66
James ch.1 v10-11

AD 96
Revelation ch.8 v7

Guilt

Most popular Old Testament	Most popular New Testament
Leviticus.	2 Timothy and Hebrews.
If the book is missing, it would be **bold** Pentateuch **Joshua and Judges** History books After captivity Psalms Proverbs and Ecclesiastes Major prophets Minor prophets	**Gospels** **Acts** Letters of Paul **Letter of James** **Letters of Peter** Pastoral Epistles Hebrews **Revelation**
Missing books Why is it not in Revelation?	
Added books Why is it in Leviticus?	
What meaning is there in the Old Testament The guilt offering is when you failed against God.	What meaning is there in the New Testament Burdened with the guilt of sin.
How many verses in the Old Testament One hundred and Four.	How many verses in the New Testament Two.

1300 BC
Job ch.6 v29-30; ch.33 v9-11

1280 BC
Exodus ch.28 v38, v43

1240 BC
Leviticus ch.5 v5-6, v15; ch.14 v13-14
Numbers ch.15 v31
Deuteronomy ch.24 v4

1000 BC
Psalm ch.32 v5
Psalm ch.51 v9-10

975 BC
2 Samuel ch.24 v10

950 BC
Proverbs ch.14 v9

720 BC
Hosea ch.5 v15

690 BC
Micah ch.7 v18

580 BC
2 Chronicles ch.28 v13
Jeremiah ch.2 v22

570 BC
Ezekiel ch.21 v24

450 BC
Ezra ch.9 v6-7

AD 64
2 Timothy ch.3 v6-7

Hanging

Most popular Old Testament	Most popular New Testament
Joshua.	Acts.
If the book is missing, it would be **bold** Pentateuch Joshua and Judges **History books** **After captivity** Psalms **Proverbs and Ecclesiastes** **Major prophets** **Minor prophets**	Gospels Acts **Letters of Paul** **Letter of James** **Letters of Peter** **Pastoral Epistles** **Hebrews** **Revelation**
Missing books Why is it not in the History Books?	
Added books Why is it in Acts?	
What meaning is there in the Old Testament Only a victim should be hung.	What meaning is there in the New Testament We find Jesus hanging on a cross.
How many verses in the Old Testament Five.	How many verses in the New Testament Five.

1300 BC
Job ch.18 v6

1240 BC
Deuteronomy ch.21 v22-23

1220 BC
Joshua ch.2 v18-19

1000 BC
Psalm ch.137 v2

AD 30
Luke ch.23 v39
John ch.19 v31

AD 63
Acts ch.5 v30; ch.10 v39-41; ch.28 v4-6

Harvest

Most popular Old Testament Leviticus.	Most popular New Testament Matthew.
If the book is missing, it would be **bold** Pentateuch Joshua and Judges History books After captivity Psalms Proverbs and Ecclesiastes Major prophets Minor prophets	Gospels **Acts** Letters of Paul Letter of James **Letters of Peter** **Pastoral Epistles** Hebrews Revelation
Missing books Why is it not in the Acts?	
Added books Why is it in the Leviticus?	
What meaning is there in the Old Testament The time of harvest will be there as the earth remains.	What meaning is there in the New Testament We can produce a harvest of good deeds for God.
How many verses in the Old Testament One hundred and Twenty-nine.	How many verses in the New Testament Forty-one.

1680 BC
Genesis ch.8 v22

1300 BC
Job ch.24 v10

1280 BC
Exodus ch.23 v10-12; ch.34 v26

1240 BC
Leviticus ch.19 v9-10
Deuteronomy ch.28 v38-39

1150 BC
Ruth ch.2 v23

1000 BC
Psalm ch.68 v10; ch.126 v6

950 BC
Proverbs ch.20 v4-5

720 BC
Hosea ch.2 v9

685 BC
Isaiah ch.24 v13-14

580 BC
2 Kings ch.19 v29
Jeremiah ch.5 v24

550 BC
Joel ch.3 v13-14

515 BC
Haggai ch.1 v9-11

AD 30
Matthew ch.6 v26-27; ch.9 v37-38; ch.13 v23, v39
John ch.4 v38

AD 53
1 Corinthians ch.9 v11-12

AD 54
Galatians ch.6 v8-10

AD 55
Romans ch.7 v4-6
2 Corinthians ch.9 v10-11

AD 66
James ch.3 v18

AD 96
Revelation ch.14 v15-16

Hope

Most popular Old Testament	Most popular New Testament
Psalms.	Romans.

If the book is missing, it would be **bold**	
Pentateuch	Gospels
Joshua and Judges	Acts
History books	Letters of Paul
After captivity	**Letter of James**
Psalms	Letters of Peter
Proverbs and Ecclesiastes	Pastoral Epistles
Major prophets	Hebrews
Minor prophets	**Revelation**

Missing books
Why is it not in Revelation?

Added books
Why is it in Jeremiah?

What meaning is there in the Old Testament	What meaning is there in the New Testament
Hope is searching for rescue.	Jesus is the hope of the world and he saved us.

How many verses in the Old Testament	How many verses in the New Testament
One hundred and Two.	Sixty-one.

1300 BC
Job ch.4 v6; ch.11 v18-20; ch.29 v13-14

1010 BC
1 Samuel ch.15 v32

1000 BC
Psalm ch.25 v21; ch.62 v5; ch.119 v74; ch.145 v15-16

950 BC
Proverbs ch.19 v18; ch.29 v20-21
Ecclesiastes ch.9 v4

750 BC
Amos ch.5 v20-21

685 BC
Isaiah ch.51 v4

580 BC
Jeremiah ch.14 v19; ch.16 v17-18; ch.31 v17-18
Lamentations ch.2 v14-15

570 BC
Ezekiel ch.7 v3-4

515 BC
Zechariah ch.9 v12-13

450 BC
Ezra ch.10 v2-3

AD 30
Matthew ch.12 v21-22

AD 49
1 Thessalonians ch.2 v19-20

AD 53
1 Corinthians ch.13 v13

AD 55
Romans ch.5 v4-5; ch.8 v24; ch.15 v4

AD 63
Acts ch.23 v6

AD 64
1 Timothy ch.4 v10
1 Peter ch.3 v15-16

AD 66
Hebrews ch.6 v19; ch.11 v1-2

Humility

Most popular Old Testament	Most popular New Testament
Proverbs.	Luke, Colossians, Titus, James and 1 Peter.
If the book is missing, it would be **bold**	
Pentateuch	Gospels
Joshua and Judges	**Acts**
History books	Letters of Paul
After captivity	Letter of James
Psalms	Letters of Peter
Proverbs and Ecclesiastes	Pastoral Epistles
Major prophets	**Hebrews**
Minor prophets	**Revelation**
Missing books Why is it not in the Major Prophets?	
Added books Why is it in 1 Peter?	
What meaning is there in the Old Testament Humility gives wisdom, honour and long life.	What meaning is there in the New Testament We should be gentle with humility.
How many verses in the Old Testament Six.	How many verses in the New Testament Five.

1000 BC
Psalm ch.45 v4

950 BC
Proverbs ch.11 v2-3; ch.15 v33; ch.18 v12-13; ch.22 v4-5; ch.29 v23-24

AD 61
Colossians ch.3 v12-13

AD 64
Titus ch.3 v2
1 Peter ch.5 v5

AD 66
James ch.3 v13-14

Inheritance

Most popular Old Testament	Most popular New Testament
Psalms.	Acts, Galatians, Ephesians and Hebrews.
If the book is missing, it would be **bold** Pentateuch Joshua and Judges History books After captivity Psalms Proverbs and Ecclesiastes Major prophets Minor prophets	**Gospels** Acts Letters of Paul **Letter of James** Letters of Peter **Pastoral Epistles** Hebrews **Revelation**
Missing books Why is it not in the Gospels?	
Added books Why is it in Psalms?	
What meaning is there in the Old Testament The firstborn son inherits his father's property.	What meaning is there in the New Testament In Jesus, we have an inheritance.
How many verses in the Old Testament Forty-three.	How many verses in the New Testament Sixteen.

1680 BC
Genesis ch.21 v10

1300 BC
Job ch.27 v13-14

1240 BC
Leviticus ch.25 v45-46
Numbers ch.27 v8-11
Deuteronomy ch.21 v16-17

1060 BC
Judges ch.11 v2

1000 BC
Psalm ch.47 v4

975 BC
2 Samuel ch.14 v15-17
1 Chronicles ch.28 v8

950 BC
Proverbs ch.13 v22-23; ch.19 v14; ch.20 v21-22

850 BC
1 Kings ch.21 v3
2 Chronicles ch.20 v11-12

690 BC
Micah ch.2 v2-3

580 BC
Jeremiah ch.3 v18
Lamentations ch.5 v2

570 BC
Ezekiel ch.46 v16-17
Obadiah ch.1 v17

530 BC
Daniel ch.12 v13

400 BC
Nehemiah ch.11 v20-21

AD 54
Galatians ch.3 v18; ch.4 v1-3

AD 61
Ephesians ch.1 v14
Colossians ch.1 v12-13; ch.3 v24

AD 63
Acts ch.20 v32

AD 64
1 Peter ch.1 v3-5

AD 66
Hebrews ch.9 v15

Jealousy

Most popular Old Testament	Most popular New Testament
Deuteronomy.	Acts, Romans, 2 Corinthians and James.
If the book is missing, it would be **bold**	**Gospels**
Pentateuch	Acts
Joshua and Judges	Letters of Paul
History books	Letter of James
After captivity	Letters of Peter
Psalms	Pastoral Epistles
Proverbs and Ecclesiastes	**Hebrews**
Major prophets	**Revelation**
Minor prophets	
Missing books Why is it not in Jeremiah?	
Added books Why is it in Deuteronomy?	
What meaning is there in the Old Testament The Lord is a jealous God.	What meaning is there in the New Testament The jealousy was while we were still sinners.
How many verses in the Old Testament Fifteen.	How many verses in the New Testament Thirteen.

1240 BC
Numbers ch.5 v25
Deuteronomy ch.29 v20; ch.32 v16, v21

1000 BC
Psalm ch.79 v5

950 BC
Proverbs ch.27 v4

685 BC
Isaiah ch.11 v13

625 BC
Zephaniah ch.1 v18; ch.3 v8

570 BC
Ezekiel ch.38 v19

AD 63
Acts ch.5 v17-19; ch.8 v23-24

AD 53
1 Corinthians ch.10 v22-24
Philippians ch.1 v15-16

AD 54
Galatians ch.5 v19-21

AD 55
2 Corinthians ch.11 v2; ch.12 v20-21
Romans ch.13 v13-14

AD 64
1 Peter ch.2 v1-2
1 Timothy ch.6 v4-5

AD 66
James ch.3 v15-16

Jew

Most popular Old Testament	Most popular New Testament
Esther.	Romans.
If the book is missing, it would be **bold**	**Gospels** Acts
Pentateuch **Joshua and Judges** **History books** After captivity **Psalms** **Proverbs and Ecclesiastes** **Major prophets** Minor prophets	Letters of Paul **Letter of James** **Letters of Peter** **Pastoral Epistles** **Hebrews** **Revelation**
Missing books Why it is not in Proverbs?	
Added books Why is it in Esther?	
What meaning is there in the Old Testament Being a Jew meant that you were kept apart.	What meaning is there in the New Testament Save everyone who believes, even a Jew.
How many verses in the Old Testament Eight.	How many verses in the New Testament Seventeen.

515 BC
Zechariah ch.8 v23

465 BC
Esther ch.3 v4; ch.10 v3

AD 30
John ch.4 v9; ch.18 v35

AD 53
1 Corinthians ch.9 v20-21

AD 54
Galatians ch.3 v28-29

AD 55
Romans ch.1 v16; ch.2 v28-29; ch.10 v12-13

AD 61
Colossians ch.3 v11

AD 63
Acts ch.19 v34-35; ch.22 v3-4

Judging

Most popular Old Testament	Most popular New Testament
Judges.	Matthew and James.
If the book is missing, it would be **bold** **Pentateuch** Joshua and Judges **History books** **After captivity** **Psalms** **Proverbs and Ecclesiastes** Major prophets **Minor prophets**	Gospels Acts **Letters of Paul** Letter of James **Letters of Peter** **Pastoral Epistles** **Hebrews** **Revelation**
Missing books Why is it not in the Letters of Paul?	
Added books Why is it in the Letter of James?	
What meaning is there in the Old Testament A judge was appointed to be fair to people.	What meaning is there in the New Testament God has arranged a time when Christ will judge all people.
How many verses in the Old Testament Two.	How many verses in the New Testament Seven.

1060 BC
Judges ch.4 v4

570 BC
Ezekiel ch.18 v8

AD 30
Matthew ch.7 v2; ch.19 v28
Luke ch.22 v30
John ch.12 v31

AD 63
Acts ch.17 v31

AD 66
James ch.4 v11-12

Key

Most popular Old Testament Deuteronomy, Judges, Proverbs and Isaiah.	Most popular New Testament Revelation.
If the book is missing, it would be **bold** Pentateuch Joshua and Judges **History books** **After captivity** **Psalms** Proverbs and Ecclesiastes Major prophets **Minor prophets**	Gospels **Acts** **Letters of Paul** **Letter of James** **Letters of Peter** **Pastoral Epistles** **Hebrews** Revelation
Missing books Why is it not in the Major Prophets?	
Added books Why is it in Revelation?	
What meaning is there in the Old Testament For the Israelites are the key to life.	What meaning is there in the New Testament The key is to guard Satan.
How many verses in the Old Testament Four.	How many verses in the New Testament Four.

1240 BC
Deuteronomy ch.30 v20

1060 BC
Judges ch.3 v25

950 BC
Proverbs ch.4 v13-14

685 BC
Isaiah ch.22 v22-23

AD 30
Luke ch.11 v52

AD 96
Revelation ch.3 v7; ch.9 v1; ch.20 v1-3

Kiss

Most popular Old Testament	Most popular New Testament
Song of Songs.	Luke.

If the book is missing, it would be **bold**	
	Gospels
Pentateuch	**Acts**
Joshua and Judges	**Letters of Paul**
History books	**Letter of James**
After captivity	**Letters of Peter**
Psalms	**Pastoral Epistles**
Proverbs and Ecclesiastes	**Hebrews**
Major prophets	**Revelation**
Minor prophets	

Missing books
Why is it not in Psalms?

Added books
Why is it only in the Gospels?

What meaning is there in the Old Testament	What meaning is there in the New Testament
The kiss is a sign of affection.	The kiss is a betrayal of Jesus.

How many verses in the Old Testament	How many verses in the New Testament
Ten.	Seven.

1680 BC
Genesis ch.27 v26; ch.31 v28-29

975 BC
2 Samuel ch.20 v9

950 BC
Proverbs ch.24 v26
Song of Songs ch.1 v2; ch.8 v1

850 BC
1 Kings ch.19 v20

720 BC
Hosea ch.13 v2

685 BC
Isaiah ch.60 v14

AD 30
Matthew ch.26 v48-49
Luke ch.7 v45; ch.22 v47-48

Leprosy

Most popular Old Testament 2 Kings.	Most popular New Testament Matthew and Luke.
If the book is missing, it would be **bold** Pentateuch **Joshua and Judges** History books **After captivity** **Psalms** **Proverbs and Ecclesiastes** **Major prophets** **Minor prophets**	Gospels **Acts** **Letters of Paul** **Letter of James** **Letters of Peter** **Pastoral Epistles** **Hebrews** **Revelation**
Missing books Why is it not in the Major Prophets?	
Added books Why is it only in the Gospels?	
What meaning is there in the Old Testament You can't be cured of leprosy.	What meaning is there in the New Testament Jesus was able to heal leprosy.
How many verses in the Old Testament Fifteen.	How many verses in the New Testament Seventeen.

1240 BC
Numbers ch.12 v10

975 BC
2 Samuel ch.3 v29

580 BC
2 Kings ch.5 v1, v27; ch.7 v3; ch.15 v5
2 Chronicles ch.26 v21

AD 30
Matthew ch.8 v2-3; ch.10 v8
Mark ch.14 v3
Luke ch.17 v12-13

Marriage

Most popular Old Testament Judges.	Most popular New Testament 1 Corinthians.
If the book is missing, it would be **bold** Pentateuch Joshua and Judges History books After captivity **Psalms** **Proverbs and Ecclesiastes** Major prophets Minor prophets	Gospels **Acts** Letters of Paul **Letter of James** **Letters of Peter** **Pastoral Epistles** Hebrews **Revelation**
Missing books Why is it not in the Proverbs?	
Added books Why is it in 1 Corinthians?	
What meaning is there in the Old Testament A father chooses one of his sons to get married.	What meaning is there in the New Testament There will be love between husband and wife.
How many verses in the Old Testament Twenty-three.	How many verses in the New Testament Seventeen.

1220 BC
Joshua ch.15 v16

1060 BC
Judges ch.3 v6; ch.14 v20; ch.21 v1

1010 BC
1 Samuel ch.18 v18-19

850 BC
1 Kings ch.11 v19

530 BC
Daniel ch.11 v6

445 BC
Malachi ch.2 v14

AD 30
Matthew ch.22 v30
Luke ch.20 v34-36

AD 53
1 Corinthians ch.7 v7, v14, v27-29

AD 55
Romans ch.7 v2-3

AD 66
Hebrews ch.13 v4

Milk

Most popular Old Testament	Most popular New Testament
Deuteronomy.	1 Corinthians and Hebrews.

If the book is missing, it would be **bold**	
Pentateuch	**Gospels**
Joshua and Judges	**Acts**
History books	Letters of Paul
After captivity	**Letter of James**
Psalms	Letters of Peter
Proverbs and Ecclesiastes	**Pastoral Epistles**
Major prophets	Hebrews
Minor prophets	**Revelation**

Missing books

Why is it not in the History Books?

Added books

Why is it in Deuteronomy?

What meaning is there in the Old Testament	What meaning is there in the New Testament
God promises to give the Israelites milk and honey.	You must feed on spiritual milk.

How many verses in the Old Testament	How many verses in the New Testament
Forty-two.	Five.

1680 BC
Genesis ch.18 v8; ch.49 v12

1300 BC
Job ch.20 v17

1280 BC
Exodus ch.33 v3

1240 BC
Leviticus ch.20 v24
Deuteronomy ch.26 v9-10

1060 BC
Judges ch.4 v19

1000 BC
Psalm ch.131 v2

950 BC
Proverbs ch.27 v27

720 BC
Hosea ch.9 v14

685 BC
Isaiah ch.7 v22; ch.55 v1

580 BC
Jeremiah ch.32 v22
Lamentations ch.4 v7

570 BC
Ezekiel ch.20 v6; ch.25 v4; ch.34 v2-4

550 BC
Joel ch.3 v18

AD 53
1 Corinthians ch.3 v2-3; ch.9 v7

AD 64
1 Peter ch.2 v2-3

AD 66
Hebrews ch.5 v12-14

Miracles

Most popular Old Testament Psalms.	Most popular New Testament Matthew.
If the book is missing, it would be **bold** Pentateuch Joshua and Judges History books After captivity Psalms **Proverbs and Ecclesiastes** Major prophets Minor prophets	Gospels Acts Letters of Paul **Letter of James** **Letters of Peter** **Pastoral Epistles** Hebrews Revelation
Missing books Why is it not in Isaiah?	
Added books Why is it in Matthew's Gospel?	
What meaning is there in the Old Testament God did miracles for his people.	What meaning is there in the New Testament The Holy Spirit helped people do miracles.
How many verses in the Old Testament Thirty-two.	How many verses in the New Testament Thirty-four.

1300 BC
Job ch.37 v14-18

1280 BC
Exodus ch.3 v20; ch.4 v21; ch.34 v10-11

1240 BC
Deuteronomy ch.13 v1-3

1220 BC
Joshua ch.24 v17

1060 BC
Judges ch.13 v23

1000 BC
Psalm ch.106 v2; ch.145 v5

975 BC
2 Samuel ch.7 v23

690 BC
Micah ch.7 v15

580 BC
Jeremiah ch.32 v20

550 BC
Joel ch.2 v26

400 BC
Nehemiah ch.9 v17

AD 30
Matthew ch.11 v20; ch.13 v54, v58
Luke ch.24 v19-21

AD 50
2 Thessalonians ch.2 v9-11

AD 53
1 Corinthians ch.12 v10-11

AD 54
Galatians ch.3 v5

AD 55
2 Corinthians ch.12 v12

AD 63
Acts ch.2 v22

AD 66
Hebrews ch.2 v4

AD 96
Revelation ch.13 v13; ch.16 v14

Nature

Most popular Old Testament	Most popular New Testament
Jeremiah.	Romans.
If the book is missing, it would be **bold** **Pentateuch** **Joshua and Judges** **History books** **After captivity** **Psalms** **Proverbs and Ecclesiastes** Major prophets **Minor prophets**	Gospels **Acts** Letters of Paul **Letter of James** Letters of Peter **Pastoral Epistles** **Hebrews** **Revelation**
Missing books Why is not in Genesis?	
Added books Why is it in Romans?	
What meaning is there in the Old Testament Nature refers to the environment.	What meaning is there in the New Testament Nature relates to avoiding sin.
How many verses in the Old Testament One.	How many verses in the New Testament Thirty-eight.

580 BC
Jeremiah ch.31 v36

AD 30
John ch.2 v24-25

AD 53
1 Corinthians ch.3 v3-4

AD 54
Galatians ch.5 v17

AD 55
Romans ch.6 v19; ch.7 v25; ch.8 v4, v8

AD 61
Ephesians ch.2 v3; ch.4 v24
Colossians ch.3 v9-11

AD 80
2 Peter ch.1 v4

Number

Most popular Old Testament Numbers.	Most popular New Testament Acts and Revelation.
If the book is missing, it would be **bold** Pentateuch Joshua and Judges History books After captivity Psalms **Proverbs and Ecclesiastes** Major prophets Minor prophets	Gospels Acts Letters of Paul **Letter of James** **Letters of Peter** **Pastoral Epistles** Hebrews Revelation
Missing books Why is it not in Isaiah?	
Added books Why is it in only in 1 Chronicles?	
What meaning is there in the Old Testament There were numerous references to number.	What meaning is there in the New Testament The number indicated the number of believers.
How many verses in the Old Testament Sixty-nine.	How many verses in the New Testament Eighteen.

1680 BC
Genesis ch.22 v17-18

1280 BC
Exodus ch.5 v19

1240 BC
Leviticus ch.25 v15-17, v50
Numbers ch.1 v20; ch.3 v49
Deuteronomy ch.25 v2-3; ch.26 v5; ch.32 v8

975 BC
1 Chronicles ch.21 v3; ch.22 v15-16

750 BC
Amos ch.5 v12-13

580 BC
Jeremiah ch.31 v27; ch.44 v28

570 BC
Ezekiel ch.4 v4

450 BC
Ezra ch.7 v34

400 BC
Nehemiah ch.5 v18

AD 30
Luke ch.5 v9-10

AD 63
Acts ch.6 v7; ch.11 v21; ch.19 v19

AD 55
Romans ch.11 v25-26

AD 96
Revelation ch.6 v11; ch.15 v2-3

Obedience

Most popular Old Testament Deuteronomy.	Most popular New Testament Romans and Philippians.
If the book is missing, it would be **bold** Pentateuch Joshua and Judges History books After captivity **Psalms** Proverbs and Ecclesiastes Major prophets Minor prophets	**Gospels** **Acts** Letters of Paul **Letter of James** **Letters of Peter** Pastoral Epistles Hebrews **Revelation**
Missing books Why is it not in the Gospels?	
Added books Why is it in Haggai?	
What meaning is there in the Old Testament They didn't obey what God told them to do.	What meaning is there in the New Testament Jesus humbled himself in obedience to God.
How many verses in the Old Testament Fifteen.	How many verses in the New Testament Six.

1060 BC
Judges ch.2 v17

1010 BC
1 Samuel ch.15 v22

975 BC
1 Chronicles ch.24 v19

580 BC
2 Kings ch.23 v24
2 Chronicles ch.27 v6

570 BC
Ezekiel ch.20 v13, v21

AD 53
Philippians ch.2 v8; ch.3 v5-6

AD 55
Romans ch.4 v13; ch.10 v5

AD 64
Titus ch.3 v9

AD 66
Hebrews ch.5 v8

Order

Most popular Old Testament	Most popular New Testament
Exodus and 2 Chronicles.	Hebrews.
If the book is missing, it would be **bold** Pentateuch Joshua and Judges History books After captivity Psalms **Proverbs and Ecclesiastes** Major prophets Minor prophets	Gospels Acts Letters of Paul **Letter of James** **Letters of Peter** **Pastoral Epistles** Hebrews **Revelation**

Missing books
Why is it not in Romans?

Added books
Why is it in Hebrews?

What meaning is there in the Old Testament	What meaning is there in the New Testament
A person of note made an order.	Everything should be done properly and in order.

How many verses in the Old Testament	How many verses in the New Testament
Fifty-eight.	Twenty-five.

1300 BC
Job ch.11 v10

1280 BC
Exodus ch.1 v15-17, v22; ch.14 v4

1240 BC
Leviticus ch.8 v34-35
Numbers ch.2 v17; ch.31 v22-24

1220 BC
Joshua ch.22 v2

1010 BC
1 Samuel ch.2 v8

1000 BC
Psalm ch.91 v11

975 BC
2 Samuel ch.17 v23
1 Chronicles ch.15 v14-15

850 BC
1 Kings ch.12 v18; ch.22 v27

685 BC
Isaiah ch.38 v1

570 BC
Ezekiel ch.21 v26

530 BC
Daniel ch.4 v6

465 BC
Esther ch.3 v4

400 BC
Nehemiah ch.5 v9

AD 30
Matthew ch.12 v44-45
Mark ch.7 v9
Luke ch.16 v2

AD 53
1 Corinthians ch.1 v27-28; ch.14 v40

AD 54
Galatians ch.1 v4-5

AD 63
Acts ch.20 v30

AD 66
Hebrews ch.6 v11; ch.10 v9-10; ch.11 v35-38

Parents

Most popular Old Testament	Most popular New Testament
Deuteronomy.	Luke.
If the book is missing, it would be **bold**	
Pentateuch	Gospels
Joshua and Judges	Acts
History books	Letters of Paul
After captivity	**Letter of James**
Psalms	**Letters of Peter**
Proverbs and Ecclesiastes	Pastoral Epistles
Major prophets	Hebrews
Minor prophets	**Revelation**
Missing books Why is it not in Isaiah?	
Added books Why is it in Deuteronomy?	
What meaning is there in the Old Testament Parents are linked to discipline.	What meaning is there in the New Testament Children will have to honour their parents.
How many verses in the Old Testament Thirty.	How many verses in the New Testament Thirty-eight.

1680 BC
Genesis ch.38 v11

1280 BC
Exodus ch.20 v5-6

1240 BC
Numbers ch.14 v18-19
Deuteronomy ch.21 v20-21; ch.22 v21; ch.24 v16; ch.33 v9

1150 BC
Ruth ch.1 v12-13

1000 BC
Psalm ch.78 v57

950 BC
Proverbs ch.17 v6; ch.28 v7

580 BC
Jeremiah ch.13 v14

570 BC
Ezekiel ch.5 v10; ch.18 v2-4; ch.20 v18-20

AD 30
Matthew ch.10 v21-22; ch.15 v6
Mark ch.7 v12
Luke ch.2 v22; ch.18 v15
John ch.9 v2-4, v22

AD 55
Romans ch.1 v30; ch.2 v28-29
2 Corinthians ch.12 v14

AD 61
Ephesians ch.6 v1-2
Colossians ch.3 v20

AD 63
Acts ch.7 v19-21

AD 64
1 Timothy ch.5 v4
2 Timothy ch.3 v2

AD 66
Hebrews ch.11 v23

Patience

Most popular Old Testament Psalms.	Most popular New Testament Colossians and James.
If the book is missing, it would be **bold** **Pentateuch** **Joshua and Judges** **History books** **After captivity** Psalms Proverbs and Ecclesiastes Major prophets Minor prophets	**Gospels** **Acts** Letters of Paul Letter of James Letters of Peter Pastoral Epistles Hebrews **Revelation**
Missing books Why is it not in Jeremiah and Ezekiel?	
Added books Why is it in Colossians?	
What meaning is there in the Old Testament The people of Israel tested God's patience.	What meaning is there in the New Testament Be filled with love and patience.
How many verses in the Old Testament Seven.	How many verses in the New Testament Eleven.

1000 BC
Psalm ch.78 v41; ch.95 v9; ch.106 v14

950 BC
Proverbs ch.25 v15
Ecclesiastes ch.7 v8

690 BC
Micah ch.2 v7

685 BC
Isaiah ch.7 v13

AD 54
Galatians ch.5 v22-23

AD 55
Romans ch.15 v5
2 Corinthians ch.6 v6-7

AD 61
Colossians ch.1 v11-12; ch.3 v12-13

AD 64
1 Timothy ch.1 v16-17
2 Timothy ch.3 v10-11
Titus ch.2 v2

AD 66
Hebrews ch.3 v9-11
James ch.5 v10-11

AD 80
2 Peter ch.3 v15

Poverty

Most popular Old Testament Proverbs.	Most popular New Testament 2 Corinthians and Revelation.
If the book is missing, it would be **bold** Pentateuch **Joshua and Judges** **History books** **After captivity** **Psalms** Proverbs and Ecclesiastes **Major prophets** **Minor prophets**	**Gospels** **Acts** Letters of Paul **Letter of James** **Letters of Peter** **Pastoral Epistles** **Hebrews** Revelation
Missing books Why is it not in the Psalms?	
Added books Why is it in Proverbs?	
What meaning is there in the Old Testament Poverty remained with the Israelites.	What meaning is there in the New Testament Poverty makes you rich.
How many verses in the Old Testament Twenty-two.	How many verses in the New Testament Two.

1300 BC
Job ch.21 v25

1240 BC
Leviticus ch.25 v25, v47-48

950 BC
Proverbs ch.6 v11; ch.10 v15; ch.13 v18; ch.14 v23; ch.19 v4; ch.21 v5; ch.28 v19; ch.30 v8; ch.31 v7
Ecclesiastes ch.4 v14

AD 55
2 Corinthians ch.8 v9

AD 96
Revelation ch.2 v9

Race

Most popular Old Testament	Most popular New Testament
Daniel.	Galatians and Philippians.
If the book is missing, it would be **bold** Pentateuch Joshua and Judges **History books** After captivity Psalms Proverbs and Ecclesiastes Major prophets Minor prophets	**Gospels** **Acts** Letters of Paul **Letter of James** **Letters of Peter** Pastoral Epistles Hebrews **Revelation**
Missing books Why is it not in the Gospels?	
Added books Why is it in Galatians and Philippians?	
What meaning is there in the Old Testament God set up Israel to be the race which everyone wanted.	What meaning is there in the New Testament For the Christians, the race was to get to the end.
How many verses in the Old Testament Twenty-three.	How many verses in the New Testament Seven.

1680 BC
Genesis ch.6 v7; ch.8 v21-22

1240 BC
Deuteronomy ch.32 v8

1000 BC
Psalm ch.14 v2-3; ch.33 v13-15

950 BC
Proverbs ch.6 v18
Ecclesiastes ch.1 v13-14; ch.9 v11

580 BC
Jeremiah ch.10 v14; ch.12 v5

530 BC
Daniel ch.4 v1-2; ch.7 v14

450 BC
Ezra ch.9 v2

AD 53
1 Corinthians ch.9 v24-25
Philippians ch.2 v16-17; ch.3 v14

AD 54
Galatians ch.2 v2-3; ch.5 v7-9

AD 64
2 Timothy ch.4 v7-8

AD 66
Hebrews ch.12 v1-2

Religion

Most popular Old Testament Daniel and Hosea.	Most popular New Testament Acts and James.
If the book is missing, it would be **bold** **Pentateuch** **Joshua and Judges** **History books** After captivity **Psalms** **Proverbs and Ecclesiastes** **Major prophets** Minor prophets	**Gospels** Acts Letters of Paul Letter of James **Letters of Peter** **Pastoral Epistles** Hebrews **Revelation**
Missing books Why is it not in the Major Prophets?	
Added books Why is it in James?	
What meaning is there in the Old Testament The rules of the Jewish religion.	What meaning is there in the New Testament Religion means caring for orphans and widows.
How many verses in the Old Testament Two.	How many verses in the New Testament Five.

530 BC
Daniel ch.6 v5

720 BC
Hosea ch.5 v7

AD 54
Galatians ch.1 v13-14

AD 63
Acts ch.25 v19-20; ch.26 v5

AD 66
James ch.1 v26-27

Reward

Most popular Old Testament Proverbs and Isaiah.	Most popular New Testament Matthew.
If the book is missing, it would be **bold** Pentateuch **Joshua and Judges** History books After captivity Psalms Proverbs and Ecclesiastes Major prophets Minor prophets	Gospels **Acts** Letters of Paul **Letter of James** Letters of Peter **Pastoral Epistles** Hebrews Revelation
Missing books Why is it not in Mark's Gospel?	
Added books Why is it in Matthew's Gospel?	
What meaning is there in the Old Testament Reward is like a battle won, or your wife and children.	What meaning is there in the New Testament God will reward each of us for the good we do.
How many verses in the Old Testament Fifty-five.	How many verses in the New Testament Thirty-four.

1680 BC
Genesis ch.15 v1; ch.30 v20

1240 BC
Numbers ch.24 v11

1150 BC
Ruth ch.1 v8-9

1010 BC
1 Samuel ch.17 v25; ch.25 v28; ch.26 v23-24

1000 BC
Psalm ch.19 v11; ch.91 v16; ch.127 v3

950 BC
Proverbs ch.11 v18, v23
Ecclesiastes ch.9 v5-6, v9-10

690 BC
Micah ch.2 v3

685 BC
Isaiah ch.40 v10; ch.61 v8

580 BC
Jeremiah ch.31 v16

AD 30
Matthew ch.5 v12; ch.6 v6
Luke ch.6 v35-36; ch.14 v14

AD 61
Ephesians ch.6 v8

AD 64
1 Peter ch.1 v9, v17; ch.3 v14-15

AD 66
Hebrews ch.10 v35-36

AD 93
2 John ch.1 v8-9

AD 96
Revelation ch.11 v18; ch.22 v12

Salt

Most popular Old Testament Leviticus and 2 Kings.	Most popular New Testament Matthew.
If the book is missing, it would be **bold** Pentateuch Joshua and Judges History books After captivity Psalms **Proverbs and Ecclesiastes** Major prophets Minor prophets	Gospels **Acts** **Letters of Paul** **Letter of James** **Letters of Peter** **Pastoral Epistles** **Hebrews** **Revelation**
Missing books Why is it not in Isaiah?	
Added books Why is it in the Gospels?	
What meaning is there in the Old Testament Salt is used to make things better.	What meaning is there in the New Testament Flavourless salt is thrown away.
How many verses in the Old Testament Twenty.	How many verses in the New Testament Seven.

1280 BC
Exodus ch.30 v35

1240 BC
Leviticus ch.2 v13
Deuteronomy ch.29 v23

1060 BC
Judges ch.9 v45

580 BC
2 Kings ch.2 v20-22
2 Chronicles ch.25 v11-12

625 BC
Zephaniah ch.2 v9

570 BC
Ezekiel ch.16 v4-5; ch.43 v24

450 BC
Ezra ch.6 v9-10

AD 30
Matthew ch.5 v13
Mark ch.9 v50
Luke ch.14 v35

Stranger

Most popular Old Testament Genesis, Job and Proverbs.	Most popular New Testament Matthew.
If the book is missing, it would be **bold** Pentateuch **Joshua and Judges** **History books** **After captivity** Psalms Proverbs and Ecclesiastes Major prophets **Minor prophets**	Gospels **Acts** **Letters of Paul** **Letter of James** **Letters of Peter** **Pastoral Epistles** **Hebrews** **Revelation**
Missing books Why is it not in Isaiah?	
Added books Why is it in Matthew's Gospel?	
What meaning is there in the Old Testament A stranger was an outcast.	What meaning is there in the New Testament Jesus was the stranger.
How many verses in the Old Testament Ten.	How many verses in the New Testament Five.

1680 BC
Genesis ch.23 v3-4; ch.42 v7

1300 BC
Job ch.19 v15-16; ch.31 v32

1240 BC
Deuteronomy ch.14 v21

1000 BC
Psalm ch.69 v8

950 BC
Proverbs ch.6 v1; ch.27 v2
Ecclesiastes ch.6 v2

580 BC
Jeremiah ch.14 v8

AD 30
Matthew ch.25 v35-36, v43-44
John ch.10 v4-5

Taxes

Most popular Old Testament	Most popular New Testament
2 Chronicles.	Luke.
If the book is missing, it would be **bold** **Pentateuch** **Joshua and Judges** History books After captivity **Psalms** **Proverbs and Ecclesiastes** **Major prophets** Minor prophets	Gospels **Acts** Letters of Paul **Letter of James** **Letters of Peter** **Pastoral Epistles** **Hebrews** **Revelation**
Missing books Why is it not in the History Books?	
Added books Why is it in Romans?	
What meaning is there in the Old Testament Taxes meant that the poor would suffer.	What meaning is there in the New Testament A Christian must pay taxes.
How many verses in the Old Testament Seven.	How many verses in the New Testament Eleven.

1010 BC
1 Samuel ch.17 v25

850 BC
1 Kings ch.12 v4

580 BC
2 Chronicles ch.24 v6

750 BC
Amos ch.5 v11

450 BC
Ezra ch.6 v8

400 BC
Nehemiah ch.5 v4-5

AD 30
Matthew ch.22 v16-17
Luke ch.3 v13; ch.19 v8; ch.23 v2

AD 55
Romans ch.13 v6-7

Temptation

Most popular Old Testament	Most popular New Testament
Judges.	Luke.

If the book is missing, it would be **bold**	
	Gospels
Pentateuch	**Acts**
Joshua and Judges	Letters of Paul
History books	Letter of James
After captivity	**Letters of Peter**
Psalms	Pastoral Epistles
Proverbs and Ecclesiastes	**Hebrews**
Major prophets	**Revelation**
Minor prophets	

Missing books
Why is it not in the Pentateuch?

Added books
Why is it in Luke's Gospel?

What meaning is there in the Old Testament	What meaning is there in the New Testament
Their gods will be a temptation to you.	Temptation is always there because we are human.

How many verses in the Old Testament	How many verses in the New Testament
One.	Fifteen.

1060 BC
Judges ch.2 v3

AD 30
Matthew ch.6 v13; ch.26 v41
Luke ch.8 v13; ch.11 v4; ch.22 v40, v46

AD 53
1 Corinthians ch.10 v13

AD 54
Galatians ch.6 v1-2

AD 64
1 Timothy ch.6 v9-10

AD 66
James ch.1 v12-15

Tradition

Most popular Old Testament 2 Chronicles and Esther.	Most popular New Testament Mark.
If the book is missing, it would be **bold** **Pentateuch** **Joshua and Judges** History books After captivity **Psalms** **Proverbs and Ecclesiastes** **Major prophets** **Minor prophets**	Gospels **Acts** Letters of Paul **Letter of James** **Letters of Peter** **Pastoral Epistles** **Hebrews** **Revelation**
Missing books Why is it not in Luke's Gospel?	
Added books Why is it in Esther?	
What meaning is there in the Old Testament Songs of sorrow have become a tradition.	What meaning is there in the New Testament The Pharisees had a lot of traditions for faith.
How many verses in the Old Testament Two.	How many verses in the New Testament Nine.

580 BC
2 Chronicles ch.32 v25

465 BC
Esther ch.9 v27

AD 30
Matthew ch.15 v2, v6-9
Mark ch.7 v9-11
John ch.7 v22

AD 50
2 Thessalonians ch.3 v6-7

Treasure

Most popular Old Testament	Most popular New Testament
Proverbs.	Matthew.

If the book is missing, it would be **bold**	
Pentateuch	Gospels
Joshua and Judges	**Acts**
History books	Letters of Paul
After captivity	Letter of James
Psalms	**Letters of Peter**
Proverbs and Ecclesiastes	Pastoral Epistles
Major prophets	**Hebrews**
Minor prophets	**Revelation**

Missing books
Why is it not in Hebrews?

Added books
Why is it in Proverbs?

What meaning is there in the Old Testament	What meaning is there in the New Testament
The treasure is the house of Israel.	The Christian's treasure is being kind to everyone.

How many verses in the Old Testament	How many verses in the New Testament
Thirty-two.	Fourteen.

1680 BC
Genesis ch.43 v23

1300 BC
Job ch.3 v21; ch.22 v25

1280 BC
Exodus ch.19 v5-6

1240 BC
Deuteronomy ch.7 v6; ch.14 v2; ch.26 v18-19

1010 BC
1 Samuel ch.25 v29-30

1000 BC
Psalm ch.119 v111-112

950 BC
Proverbs ch.2 v7; ch.10 v14; ch.18 v22

685 BC
Isaiah ch.33 v6

570 BC
Ezekiel ch.24 v16-17, v25-26
Obadiah ch.1 v6

445 BC
Malachi ch.3 v17

AD 30
Matthew ch.6 v21; ch.19 v21
Luke ch.12 v33-34

AD 55
2 Corinthians ch.4 v7

AD 64
1 Timothy ch.6 v19

AD 66
James ch.5 v3-4

Victory

Most popular Old Testament	Most popular New Testament
Psalms.	1 Corinthians and Revelation.

If the book is missing, it would be **bold**	
	Gospels
Pentateuch	**Acts**
Joshua and Judges	Letters of Paul
History books	**Letter of James**
After captivity	**Letters of Peter**
Psalms	**Pastoral Epistles**
Proverbs and Ecclesiastes	**Hebrews**
Major prophets	Revelation
Minor prophets	

Missing books
Why is it not in the Pastoral Epistles?

Added books
Why is it in Judges?

What meaning is there in the Old Testament	What meaning is there in the New Testament
Victory is the sign of the Lord's favour.	Victory is due to Jesus dying on the cross.

How many verses in the Old Testament	How many verses in the New Testament
One hundred and Eight.	Ten.

1280 BC
Exodus ch.15 v2; ch.32 v18

1240 BC
Numbers ch.21 v3
Deuteronomy ch.20 v4

1220 BC
Joshua ch.24 v12-13

1000 BC
Psalm ch.20 v5; ch.44 v3; ch.67 v7

975 BC
2 Samuel ch.19 v2-4
1 Chronicles ch.11 v14; ch.29 v11

950 BC
Proverbs ch.21 v31

850 BC
1 Kings ch.5 v3-4

685 BC
Isaiah ch.41 v25

570 BC
Ezekiel ch.39 v13

465 BC
Esther ch.9 v17

AD 53
1 Corinthians ch.15 v54-57

AD 55
Romans ch.8 v37

AD 61
Colossians ch.2 v15

AD 93
1 John ch.4 v4-5; ch.5 v4-5

AD 96
Revelation ch.6 v2

Vine

Most popular Old Testament	Most popular New Testament
Ezekiel.	John.

If the book is missing, it would be **bold**	
	Gospels
Pentateuch	**Acts**
Joshua and Judges	**Letters of Paul**
History books	**Letter of James**
After captivity	**Letters of Peter**
Psalms	**Pastoral Epistles**
Proverbs and Ecclesiastes	**Hebrews**
Major prophets	**Revelation**
Minor prophets	

Missing books	
Why is it not in the Psalms?	

Added books	
Why is it in John's Gospel?	

What meaning is there in the Old Testament	What meaning is there in the New Testament
A vine is like Israel.	Jesus is like a vine.

How many verses in the Old Testament	How many verses in the New Testament
Twenty-two.	Three.

1680 BC
Genesis ch.49 v11

1300 BC
Job ch.15 v33

720 BC
Hosea ch.10 v1

685 BC
Isaiah ch.24 v13

630 BC
Nahum ch.2 v2

580 BC
Jeremiah ch.2 v21

570 BC
Ezekiel ch.17 v9

445 BC
Malachi ch.3 v11-12

AD 30
John ch.15 v4-5

Wild

Most popular Old Testament	Most popular New Testament
Genesis.	Romans.

If the book is missing, it would be **bold**	
	Gospels
Pentateuch	Acts
Joshua and Judges	Letters of Paul
History books	**Letter of James**
After captivity	Letters of Peter
Psalms	Pastoral Epistles
Proverbs and Ecclesiastes	**Hebrews**
Major prophets	Revelation
Minor prophets	

Missing books
Why is it not in Hebrews?

Added books
Why is it in Job?

What meaning is there in the Old Testament	What meaning is there in the New Testament
Wild animals were made by God.	It is wild living that the Christian should shun.

How many verses in the Old Testament	How many verses in the New Testament
One hundred and Fifty-three.	Sixteen.

1680 BC
Genesis ch.1 v25, v30-31; ch.2 v19-20; ch.7 v21-23; ch.8 v1

1300 BC
Job ch.5 v22-23

1280 BC
Exodus ch.22 v31; ch.23 v11, v29

1240 BC
Leviticus ch.22 v8; ch.26 v22
Deuteronomy ch.32 v24

1000 BC
Psalm ch.68 v30; ch.147 v9

975 BC
2 Samuel ch.21 v10-11

720 BC
Hosea ch.2 v12, v18

685 BC
Isaiah ch.18 v6; ch.43 v20; ch.56 v9

625 BC
Zephaniah ch.2 v15

580 BC
Jeremiah ch.7 v33-34; ch.12 v4

570 BC
Ezekiel ch.5 v17; ch.14 v15-16; ch.33 v27

550 BC
Joel ch.1 v20

530 BC
Daniel ch.2 v38

AD 30
Luke ch.15 v13

AD 53
1 Corinthians ch.15 v32

AD 55
Romans ch.13 v13-14

AD 63
Acts ch.11 v6-7

AD 64
Titus ch.1 v6-7
1 Peter ch.4 v4

AD 96
Revelation ch.6 v8

Wrath

Most popular Old Testament	Most popular New Testament
Psalms.	Revelation.
If the book is missing, it would be **bold** Pentateuch **Joshua and Judges** **History books** After captivity Psalms Proverbs and Ecclesiastes Major prophets Minor prophets	Gospels **Acts** Letters of Paul **Letter of James** **Letters of Peter** **Pastoral Epistles** **Hebrews** Revelation
Missing books Why is it not in Ezekiel?	
Added books Why is it in Revelation?	
What meaning is there in the Old Testament God's wrath directed against Israel.	What meaning is there in the New Testament God's wrath against evil is the judgement.
How many verses in the Old Testament Sixteen.	How many verses in the New Testament Fourteen.

1000 BC
Psalm ch.78 v21-22; ch.85 v5; ch.90 v11

950 BC
Proverbs ch.27 v4

685 BC
Isaiah ch.63 v5

580 BC
Jeremiah ch.10 v10

630 BC
Nahum ch.1 v2-3

400 BC
Nehemiah ch.13 v18

AD 30
Matthew ch.3 v7-8

AD 55
Romans ch.2 v8-9

AD 96
Revelation ch.6 v17; ch.14 v19-20

Section 2

Becoming a Christian

Being a Christian

When Jesus and the apostles spoke about faith and truth, they didn't have the New Testament, and they had to rely on the Old Testament. It will be helpful, not to rely on the New Testament but to see how the Old Testament shapes the fact that God loves us, and that Jesus would die, and be raised again.

Some Christians discount the Old Testament with its history and its prophecy as being Jewish and not relevant for today, but they are totally wrong. God in his wisdom, has produced our Bibles and the Old Testament and the New Testament are all joined together, and makes certain of our faith. We have one book, the Bible.

Too often we only rely on the New Testament, but we fail to see how God's plan was there in the beginning.

	Genesis	Psalms	Isaiah
There is a God	ch.1 v1	ch.24 v1	ch.6 v1
God is good	ch.1 v31	ch.111 v7	ch.12 v2
We are sinful	ch.3 v17	ch.51 v3-5	ch.1 v4
God is love	ch.2 v8-9	ch.25 v9	ch.4 v4
God sent his son	ch.49 v10	ch.2 v6	ch.53 v1-9
Jesus died for our sins	ch.22 v15-18	ch.22 v12-18	ch.53 v10-12
There is life after death	ch.18 v19	ch.23 v4	ch.66 v22-24
The Lord will return again	ch.50 v19-21	ch.17 v15	ch.66 v18
What we do now matters	ch.5 v24	ch.33 v13-15	ch.63 v4-6
There will be a judgement	ch.6 v5	ch.9 v8	ch.3 v13-15
We can be forgiven	ch.17 v1-2	ch.32 v5	ch.1 v18
We need to respond	ch.15 v1	ch.16 v8	ch.65 v2-4
We have to change	ch.18 v18-19	ch.121 v5-8	ch.3 v10

There is a God

In the beginning God created the heavens and the earth. Genesis ch.1 v1

The earth is the Lord's, and everything in it. The world and all its people belong to him. For he laid the earth's foundation on the seas and built it on the ocean depths. Psalm ch.24 v1

It was in the year King Uzziah died that I saw the Lord. He was sitting on a lofty throne, and the train of his robe filled the Temple. Isaiah ch.6 v1

God is good

God looked over all he had made, and he saw that it was very good! Genesis ch.1 v31

All he does is just and good, and all his commandments are trustworthy. Psalm ch.111 v7

See, God has come to save me. I will trust in him and not be afraid. Isaiah ch.12 v2

We are sinful

Since you listened to your wife and ate from the tree whose fruit I commanded you not to eat, the ground is cursed because of you. All your life you will struggle to scratch a living from it. Genesis ch.3 v17

For I recognise my rebellion; it haunts me day and night. Against you, and you alone, have I sinned; I have done what is evil in your sight. You will be proved right in what you say, and your judgement against me is just. For I was born a sinner—yes, from the moment my mother conceived me. Psalm ch.51 v3-5

Oh, what a sinful nation they are—loaded down with a burden of guilt. They are evil people, corrupt children who have rejected the

*Lord. They have despised the Holy One of Israel and turned their
backs on him. Isaiah ch.1 v4*

God is love
*Then the Lord God planted a garden in Eden in the east, and there
he placed the man he had made. The Lord God made all sorts of
trees grow up from the ground—trees that were beautiful and that
produced delicious fruit. Genesis ch.2 v8-9*

*He leads the humble in doing right, teaching them his way. Psalm
ch.25 v9*

*The Lord will wash the filth from beautiful Zion and cleanse
Jerusalem of its bloodstains with the hot breath of fiery judgement.
Isaiah ch.4 v4*

God sent his son
*The sceptre will not depart from Judah, nor the ruler's staff from his
descendants, until the coming of the one to whom it belongs, the one
whom all nations will honour. Genesis ch.49 v10*

*For the Lord declares, "I have placed my chosen king on the throne
in Jerusalem, on my holy mountain." Psalm ch.2 v6*

*Who has believed our message? To whom has the Lord revealed
his powerful arm? My servant grew up in the Lord's presence like
a tender green shoot, like a root in dry ground. There was nothing
beautiful or majestic about his appearance, nothing to attract us to
him. He was despised and rejected—a man of sorrows, acquainted
with deepest grief. We turned our backs on him and looked the other
way. He was despised, and we did not care. Yet it was our weaknesses
he carried; it was our sorrows that weighed him down. And we
thought his troubles were a punishment from God, a punishment for
his own sins! But he was pierced for our rebellion, crushed for our
sins. He was beaten so we could be whole. He was whipped so we*

*could be healed. All of us, like sheep, have strayed away. We have
left God's paths to follow our own. Yet the Lord laid on him the sins
of us all. He was oppressed and treated harshly, yet he never said a
word. He was led like a lamb to the slaughter. And as a sheep is silent
before the shearers, he did not open his mouth. Unjustly condemned,
he was led away. No one cared that he died without descendants,
that his life was cut short in midstream. But he was struck down for
the rebellion of my people. He had done no wrong and had never
deceived anyone. But he was buried like a criminal; he was put in a
rich man's grave. Isaiah ch.53 v1-9*

Jesus died for our sins
*Then the angel of the Lord called again to Abraham from heaven.
"This is what the Lord says: Because you have obeyed me and have
not withheld even your son, your only son, I swear by my own name
that I will certainly bless you. I will multiply your descendants beyond
number, like the stars in the sky and the sand on the seashore."
Genesis ch.22 v15-18*

*My enemies surround me like a herd of bulls; fierce bulls of Bashan
have hemmed me in! Like lions they open their jaws against me,
roaring and tearing into their prey. My life is poured out like water,
and all my bones are out of joint. My heart is like wax, melting within
me. My strength has dried up like sunbaked clay. My tongue sticks
to the roof of my mouth. You have laid me in the dust and left me
for dead. My enemies surround me like a pack of dogs; an evil gang
closes in on me. They have pierced my hands and feet. I can count
all my bones. My enemies stare at me and gloat. They divide my
garments among themselves and throw dice for my clothing. Psalm
ch.22 v12-18*

*But it was the Lord's good plan to crush him and cause him grief.
Yet when his life is made an offering for sin, he will have many
descendants. He will enjoy a long life, and the Lord's good plan
will prosper in his hands. When he sees all that is accomplished
by his anguish, he will be satisfied. And because of his experience,*

my righteous servant will make it possible for many to be counted righteous, for he will bear all their sins. I will give him the honours of a victorious soldier, because he exposed himself to death. He was counted among the rebels. He bore the sins of many and interceded for rebels. Isaiah ch.53 v10-12

There is life after death
I have singled him out so that he will direct his sons and their families to keep the way of the Lord by doing what is right and just. Then I will do for Abraham all that I have promised. Genesis ch.18 v19

Even when I walk through the darkest valley, I will not be afraid, for you are close beside me. Your rod and your staff protect and comfort me. Psalm ch.23 v4

"As surely as my new heavens and earth will remain, so will you always be my people, with a name that will never disappear," says the Lord. "All humanity will come to worship me from week to week and from month to month. And as they go out, they will see the dead bodies of those who have rebelled against me. For the worms that devour them will never die, and the fire that burns them will never go out. All who pass by will view them with utter horror." Isaiah ch.66 v22-24

The Lord will return again
But Joseph replied, "Don't be afraid of me. Am I God, that I can punish you? You intended to harm me, but God intended it all for good. He brought me to this position so I could save the lives of many people. No, don't be afraid. I will continue to take care of you and your children." So he reassured them by speaking kindly to them. Genesis ch.50 v19-21

Because I am righteous, I will see you. When I awake, I will see you face to face and be satisfied. Psalm ch.17 v15

I can see what they are doing, and I know what they are thinking. So I will gather all nations and peoples together, and they will see my glory. Isaiah ch.66 v18-19

What we do now matters
Walking in close fellowship with God. Then one day he disappeared, because God took him. Genesis ch.5 v24

The Lord looks down from heaven and sees the whole human race. From his throne he observes all who live on the earth. He made their hearts, so he understands everything they do. Psalm ch.33 v13-15

For the time has come for me to avenge my people, to ransom them from their oppressors. I was amazed to see that no one intervened to help the oppressed. So I myself stepped in to save them with my strong arm, and my wrath sustained me. I crushed the nations in my anger and made them stagger and fall to the ground, spilling their blood upon the earth. Isaiah ch.63 v4-6

There will be a judgement
The Lord observed the extent of human wickedness on the earth, and he saw that everything they thought or imagined was consistently and totally evil. Genesis ch.6 v5-6

He will judge the world with justice and rule the nations with fairness. Psalm ch.9 v8

The Lord takes his place in court and presents his case against his people! The Lord comes forward to pronounce judgement on the elders and rulers of his people: "You have ruined Israel, my vineyard. Your houses are filled with things stolen from the poor. How dare you crush my people, grinding the faces of the poor into the dust?" demands the Lord, the Lord of Heaven's Armies. Isaiah ch.3 v13-15

We can be forgiven
The Lord appeared to him and said, "I am El-Shaddai—'God Almighty.' Serve me faithfully and live a blameless life. I will make a covenant with you, by which I will guarantee to give you countless descendants." Genesis ch.17 v1-2

Finally, I confessed all my sins to you and stopped trying to hide my guilt. I said to myself, "I will confess my rebellion to the Lord." And you forgave me! All my guilt is gone. Psalm ch.32 v5

"Come now, let's settle this," says the Lord. "Though your sins are like scarlet, I will make them as white as snow. Though they are red like crimson, I will make them as white as wool." Isaiah ch.1 v18

We need to respond
Some time later, the Lord spoke to Abram in a vision and said to him, "Do not be afraid, Abram, for I will protect you, and your reward will be great." Genesis ch.15 v1

I know the Lord is always with me. I will not be shaken, for he is right beside me. Psalm ch.16 v8

All day long I opened my arms to a rebellious people. But they follow their own evil paths and their own crooked schemes. All day long they insult me to my face by worshipping idols in their sacred gardens. They burn incense on pagan altars. At night they go out among the graves, worshipping the dead. They eat the flesh of pigs and make stews with other forbidden foods. Isaiah ch.65 v2-4

We have to change
For Abraham will certainly become a great and mighty nation, and all the nations of the earth will be blessed through him. I have singled him out so that he will direct his sons and their families to keep the way of the Lord by doing what is right and just. Then I will do for Abraham all that I have promised. Genesis ch.18 v18-19

The Lord himself watches over you! The Lord stands beside you as your protective shade. The sun will not harm you by day, nor the moon at night. The Lord keeps you from all harm and watches over your life. The Lord keeps watch over you as you come and go, both now and forever. Psalm ch.121 v5-8

Tell the godly that all will be well for them. They will enjoy the rich reward they have earned! Isaiah ch.3 v10

Section 3

No Differences between the Old Testament and New Testament

Age

Most popular Old Testament	Most popular New Testament
Genesis.	Luke.

If the book is missing, it would be **bold**	
	Gospels
Pentateuch	**Acts**
Joshua and Judges	Letters of Paul
History books	**Letter of James**
After captivity	**Letters of Peter**
Psalms	**Pastoral Epistles**
Proverbs and Ecclesiastes	Hebrews
Major prophets	**Revelation**
Minor prophets	

Missing books
Why is it in Exodus and Revelation?

Added books
Why is it in Genesis?

What meaning is there in the Old and New Testament
When you get older, the more wisdom you can expect.

How many verses in the Old Testament	How many verses in the New Testament
Forty-six.	Nine.

1680 BC
Genesis ch.15 v15; ch.25 v8-9; ch.48 v10

1300 BC
Job ch.32 v7

1240 BC
Leviticus ch.27 v4-8
Numbers ch.8 v24-26

1150 BC
Ruth ch.4 v15

1000 BC
Psalm ch.92 v14

850 BC
1 Kings ch.11 v4-5; ch.15 v23-24

975 BC
1 Chronicles ch.26 v13

685 BC
Isaiah ch.46 v4

AD 30
Matthew ch.28 v20
Luke ch.2 v37; ch.20 v35-36

AD 55
Romans ch.4 v19

AD 54
Galatians ch.4 v2-3

Almighty

Most popular Old Testament	Most popular New Testament
Job.	Revelation.

If the book is missing, it would be **bold**	
Pentateuch	**Gospels**
Joshua and Judges	**Acts**
History books	Letters of Paul
After captivity	**Letter of James**
Psalms	**Letters of Peter**
Proverbs and Ecclesiastes	Pastoral Epistles
Major prophets	**Hebrews**
Minor prophets	Revelation

Missing books
Why is it not in the Gospels?

Added books
Why is it in Job more than any other book?

What meaning is there in the Old and New Testament
God reigns over all the world.

How many verses in the Old Testament	How many verses in the New Testament
Fifty-three.	Eleven.

1680 BC
Genesis ch.17 v1-2

1300 BC
Job ch.8 v5; ch.37 v23

1280 BC
Exodus ch.6 v2-4
Numbers ch.24 v16

1000 BC
Psalm ch.91 v1

850 BC
1 Kings ch.18 v15

AD 55
2 Corinthians ch.6 v18

AD 64
1 Timothy ch.6 v15-16

AD 96
Revelation ch.1 v8; ch.4 v8; ch.15 v3-4; ch.19 v6-7; ch.21 v22

Amen

Most popular Old Testament	Most popular New Testament
Deuteronomy.	Revelation.

If the book is missing, it would be **bold**	
Pentateuch	Gospels
Joshua and Judges	**Acts**
History books	Letters of Paul
After captivity	**Letter of James**
Psalms	Letters of Peter
Proverbs and Ecclesiastes	Pastoral Epistles
Major prophets	Hebrews
Minor prophets	Revelation

Missing books

Why is it not in Genesis and Exodus?

Added books

Why is it in Revelation?

What meaning is there in the Old and New Testament

Our amen (which means 'yes') ascends to God for his glory.

How many verses in the Old Testament	How many verses in the New Testament
Twenty-six.	Twenty-eight.

1240 BC
Deuteronomy ch.27 v26

1000 BC
Psalm ch.41 v13

975 BC
1 Chronicles ch.16 v36

850 BC
1 Kings ch.1 v36-37

580 BC
Jeremiah ch.11 v4-5; ch.28 v6-7

400 BC
Nehemiah ch.5 v13

AD 49
1 Thessalonians ch.3 v13

AD 53
Philippians ch.4 v20

AD 55
Romans ch.1 v25-26; ch.9 v5; ch.11 v36
2 Corinthians ch.1 v20

AD 64
1 Timothy ch.1 v17; ch.6 v16

AD 96
Revelation ch.3 v14; ch.5 v14; ch.7 v12; ch.19 v4

Ambassador

Most popular Old Testament	Most popular New Testament
Jeremiah and Obadiah.	Ephesians.

If the book is missing, it would be **bold**	
	Gospels
Pentateuch	**Acts**
Joshua and Judges	Letters of Paul
History books	**Letter of James**
After captivity	**Letters of Peter**
Psalms	**Pastoral Epistles**
Proverbs and Ecclesiastes	**Hebrews**
Major prophets	**Revelation**
Minor prophets	

Missing books
Why is it not in the History Books?

Added books
Why is it in Ephesians?

What meaning is there in the Old and New Testament
God's ambassador was used to assemble the fighting against Edom.

How many verses in the Old Testament	How many verses in the New Testament
Two.	One.

850 BC
Jeremiah ch.49 v14

570 BC
Obadiah ch.1 v1

AD 61
Ephesians ch.6 v20

Angel

Most popular Old Testament	Most popular New Testament
Zechariah.	Revelation.

If the book is missing, it would be **bold**	
Pentateuch	Gospels
Joshua and Judges	Acts
History books	Letters of Paul
After captivity	**Letter of James**
Psalms	**Letters of Peter**
Proverbs and Ecclesiastes	**Pastoral Epistles**
Major prophets	Hebrews
Minor prophets	Revelation

Missing books

Why is it not in Deuteronomy?

Added books

Why is it in Judges and Zechariah?

What meaning is there in the Old and New Testament

The angels are messengers of God, and they can do mighty things.

How many verses in the Old Testament	How many verses in the New Testament
One hundred and Sixteen.	One hundred and Eighteen.

1680 BC
Genesis ch.16 v9-10; ch.19 v21-22; ch.21 v17-18; ch.22 v15-16; ch.24 v40

1280 BC
Exodus ch.3 v2-3; ch.12 v23; ch.14 v19-20; ch.23 v20-21
Numbers ch.20 v16; ch.22 v22

1060 BC
Judges ch.2 v4-5; ch.6 v12; ch.13 v16

1000 BC
Psalm ch.34 v7; ch.89 v6

975 BC
2 Samuel ch.14 v17; ch.24 v16

850 BC
1 Kings ch.19 v7

580 BC
2 Kings ch.1 v15; ch.19 v35

530 BC
Daniel ch.3 v28-29; ch.6 v22

515 BC
Zechariah ch.1 v13

AD 30
Matthew ch.1 v20-21; ch.2 v13; ch.28 v2-4
Luke ch.1 v19-20; ch.2 v13-15; ch.22 v43-44

AD 63
Acts ch.5 v18-19; ch.8 v26-27, ch.10 v4-6; ch.12 v7-8; ch.12 v23; ch.27
v23-24

AD 53
1 Corinthians ch.10 v10-11

AD 55
2 Corinthians ch.11 v14-15

AD 96
Revelation ch.3 v14; ch.8 v5; ch.10 v5-6; ch.14 v18-19; ch.17 v3; ch.20 v3; ch.22 v6, v8-9

Antichrist

Most popular Old Testament	Most popular New Testament
None.	Letters of John.

If the book is missing, it would be **bold**	
	Gospels
Pentateuch	**Acts**
Joshua and Judges	**Letters of Paul**
History books	**Letter of James**
After captivity	**Letters of Peter**
Psalms	**Pastoral Epistles**
Proverbs and Ecclesiastes	**Hebrews**
Major prophets	**Revelation**
Minor prophets	

Missing books
Why is it not in the Gospels?

Added books
Why is it in the Letters of John?

What meaning is there in the Old and New Testament
The antichrist will be coming; it will be a deceiver from the truth.

How many verses in the Old Testament	How many verses in the New Testament
None.	Four.

AD 93
1 John ch.2 v18-19; ch.2 v22-23; ch.4 v3
2 John ch.7 v9

Apostle

Most popular Old Testament	Most popular New Testament
None.	1 Corinthians.

If the book is missing, it would be **bold**	
Pentateuch	**Gospels**
Joshua and Judges	Acts
History books	Letters of Paul
After captivity	**Letter of James**
Psalms	Letters of Peter
Proverbs and Ecclesiastes	Pastoral Epistles
Major prophets	**Hebrews**
Minor prophets	**Revelation**

Missing books

Why is it not in the Old Testament?

Added books

Why is it in 1 Corinthians?

What meaning is there in the Old and New Testament

God has appointed some people to be apostles.

How many verses in the Old Testament	How many verses in the New Testament
None.	Twenty-five.

AD 63
Acts ch.1 v26; ch.12 v2-3

AD 53
1 Corinthians ch.9 v2

AD 54
Galatians ch.1 v19-20

AD 55
Romans ch.11 v13
2 Corinthians ch.12 v12-13

AD 64
1 Timothy ch.2 v7
2 Timothy ch.1 v11
Titus ch.1 v1

AD 80
2 Peter ch.1 v1

Ashes

Most popular Old Testament	Most popular New Testament
Numbers, Leviticus and Job.	Matthew, Luke, Hebrews and 2 Peter.

If the book is missing, it would be **bold**	
Pentateuch	Gospels
Joshua and Judges	**Acts**
History books	**Letters of Paul**
After captivity	**Letter of James**
Psalms	Letters of Peter
Proverbs and Ecclesiastes	**Pastoral Epistles**
Major prophets	Hebrews
Minor prophets	**Revelation**

Missing books

Why is it not in the Letters of Paul?

Added books

Why is it in Job?

What meaning is there in the Old and New Testament

The Israelites would lay in burlap and ashes while they would mourn.

How many verses in the Old Testament	How many verses in the New Testament
Thirty-four.	Four.

1680 BC
Genesis ch.18 v27-28

1240 BC
Leviticus ch.6 v10-12
Numbers ch.4 v13-14; ch.19 v10

1000 BC
Psalm ch.102 v9-10

975 BC
2 Samuel ch.13 v19

750 BC
Jonah ch.3 v6-7

620 BC
Habakkuk ch.2 v13

580 BC
2 Kings ch.23 v4-5
Jeremiah ch.6 v26

570 BC
Ezekiel ch.27 v30

530 BC
Daniel ch.9 v3

465 BC
Esther ch.4 v3

AD 30
Matthew ch.11 v21

AD 66
Hebrews ch.9 v13-14

AD 80
2 Peter ch.2 v6-7

Assurance

Most popular Old Testament	Most popular New Testament
Job.	Colossians.

If the book is missing, it would be **bold**	
	Gospels
Pentateuch	**Acts**
Joshua and Judges	Letters of Paul
History books	**Letter of James**
After captivity	**Letters of Peter**
Psalms	**Pastoral Epistles**
Proverbs and Ecclesiastes	Hebrews
Major prophets	**Revelation**
Minor prophets	

Missing books
Why is it only one verse in the Old Testament?

Added books
Why is it in Colossians?

What meaning is there in the Old and New Testament
Christ lives within you and the assurance we have is the Good News.

How many verses in the Old Testament	How many verses in the New Testament
One.	Four.

1300 BC
Job ch.24 v22-24

AD 49
1 Thessalonians ch.1 v5

AD 61
Colossians ch.1 v23, v27

AD 66
Hebrews ch.11 v1-2

Atonement

Most popular Old Testament	Most popular New Testament
Exodus.	Hebrews.

If the book is missing, it would be **bold**	
Pentateuch	**Gospels**
Joshua and Judges	**Acts**
History books	**Letters of Paul**
After captivity	**Letter of James**
Psalms	**Letters of Peter**
Proverbs and Ecclesiastes	**Pastoral Epistles**
Major prophets	Hebrews
Minor prophets	**Revelation**

Missing books
Why is it not in the New Testament (except in Hebrews) ?

Added books
Why is it in Exodus?

What meaning is there in the Old and New Testament
The place of the ark above the atonement cover is where God will speak to his high priest.

How many verses in the Old Testament	How many verses in the New Testament
Forty-one.	One.

1280 BC
Exodus ch.25 v17; ch.25 v21-22

1240 BC
Leviticus ch.16 v2, v13-14; ch.23 v26-28

950 BC
Proverbs ch.16 v6

975 BC
1 Chronicles ch.6 v49

580 BC
2 Chronicles ch.29 v24

570 BC
Ezekiel ch.45 v15-16

AD 66
Hebrews ch.9 v5

Authority

Most popular Old Testament	Most popular New Testament
Daniel.	Matthew.

If the book is missing, it would be **bold**	
	Gospels
Pentateuch	Acts
Joshua and Judges	Letters of Paul
History books	**Letter of James**
After captivity	Letters of Peter
Psalms	Pastoral Epistles
Proverbs and Ecclesiastes	Hebrews
Major prophets	Revelation
Minor prophets	

Missing books
Why is it not in Exodus?

Added books
Why is it in Daniel?

What meaning is there in the Old and New Testament
God has the authority and he can decide what he wants to do.

How many verses in the Old Testament	How many verses in the New Testament
Thirty-six.	One hundred and Twenty-four.

1240 BC
Numbers ch.27 v20-21

1000 BC
Psalm ch.89 v24; ch.118 v10

580 BC
2 Kings ch.23 v3
Jeremiah ch.23 v36

530 BC
Daniel ch.7 v14

515 BC
Zechariah ch.10 v12

AD 30
Matthew ch.7 v29; ch.9 v6; ch.10 v1-2
John ch.5 v22-23; ch.10 v18

AD 53
1 Corinthians ch.11 v10; ch.15 v28

AD 55
2 Corinthians ch.2 v17
Romans ch.13 v1-2

AD 61
Ephesians ch.1 v10-11
Colossians ch.2 v10

AD 64
1 Peter ch.2 v13-14

Banner

Most popular Old Testament	Most popular New Testament
Numbers.	None.

If the book is missing, it would be **bold**	
	Gospels
Pentateuch	**Acts**
Joshua and Judges	**Letters of Paul**
History books	**Letter of James**
After captivity	**Letters of Peter**
Psalms	**Pastoral Epistles**
Proverbs and Ecclesiastes	**Hebrews**
Major prophets	**Revelation**
Minor prophets	

Missing books
Why is it not in the New Testament?

Added books
Why is it in Numbers?

What meaning is there in the Old and New Testament
The banner is a victory, or a banner of salvation.

How many verses in the Old Testament	How many verses in the New Testament
Twelve.	None.

1280 BC
Exodus ch.17 v15-16

1240 BC
Numbers ch.1 v52; ch.2 v17

1000 BC
Psalm ch.20 v5; ch.60 v4

685 BC
Isaiah ch.11 v10; ch.30 v17

570 BC
Ezekiel ch.27 v7

Banquet

Most popular Old Testament	Most popular New Testament
Esther.	Luke.
If the book is missing, it would be **bold**	
Pentateuch	Gospels
Joshua and Judges	**Acts**
History books	**Letters of Paul**
After captivity	**Letter of James**
Psalms	**Letters of Peter**
Proverbs and Ecclesiastes	**Pastoral Epistles**
Major prophets	**Hebrews**
Minor prophets	Revelation
Missing books Why is it not in John's Gospel?	
Added books Why is it in Esther?	
What meaning is there in the Old and New Testament A banquet was to celebrate and there was feasting and wine.	
How many verses in the Old Testament Twenty-four.	How many verses in the New Testament Ten.

1680 BC
Genesis ch.40 v20

950 BC
Proverbs ch.9 v2
Song of Songs ch.2 v4

850 BC
I Kings ch.1 v41; ch.3 v15

685 BC
Isaiah ch.25 v6

580 BC
2 Chronicles ch.18 v2

570 BC
Ezekiel ch.39 v20

530 BC
Daniel ch.5 v10

465 BC
Esther ch.1 v3-4, v9; ch.5 v5

AD 30
Matthew ch.22 v3
Luke ch.5 v29-30; ch.14 v12-15, v24

AD 96
Revelation ch.19 v17-18

Baptism

Most popular Old Testament None.	Most popular New Testament Acts.
If the book is missing, it would be **bold** **Pentateuch** **Joshua and Judges** **History books** **After captivity** **Psalms** **Proverbs and Ecclesiastes** **Major prophets** **Minor prophets**	Gospels Acts Letters of Paul **Letter of James** Letters of Peter **Pastoral Epistles** **Hebrews** **Revelation**
Missing books Why is it not in the Old Testament?	
Added books Why is it in Acts?	
What meaning is there in the Old and New Testament John's baptism was repentance, but Jesus' baptism was to believe in him.	
How many verses in the Old Testament None.	How many verses in the New Testament Twenty-one.

AD 30
Matthew ch.3 v16-17
Mark ch.10 v38
Luke ch.3 v7-8; ch.7 v30, ch.12 v50-52

AD 54
Galatians ch.3 v27-29
Ephesians ch.4 v5-6

AD 55
Romans ch.6 v3-4

AD 63
Acts ch.10 v37-38; ch.18 v25-26; ch.19 v3-4

AD 64
1 Peter ch.3 v21

AD 93
1 John ch.5 v6-7

Beard

Most popular Old Testament	Most popular New Testament
2 Samuel.	None.

If the book is missing, it would be **bold**	
	Gospels
Pentateuch	**Acts**
Joshua and Judges	**Letters of Paul**
History books	**Letter of James**
After captivity	**Letters of Peter**
Psalms	**Pastoral Epistles**
Proverbs and Ecclesiastes	**Hebrews**
Major prophets	**Revelation**
Minor prophets	

Missing books
Why is it not in the New Testament?

Added books
Why is it in 2 Samuel?

What meaning is there in the Old and New Testament
In the Old Testament having a beard was common.

How many verses in the Old Testament	How many verses in the New Testament
Nine.	None.

1240 BC
Leviticus ch.14 v9

1010 BC
1 Samuel ch.10 v4

1000 BC
Psalm ch.133 v2

975 BC
2 Samuel ch.10 v4; ch.19 v24-25; ch.20 v9-10

685 BC
Isaiah ch.50 v6

570 BC
Ezekiel ch.5 v1

450 BC
Ezra ch.9 v3-4

Beast

Most popular Old Testament	Most popular New Testament
Daniel.	Revelation.

If the book is missing, it would be **bold**	
Pentateuch	**Gospels**
Joshua and Judges	**Acts**
History books	**Letters of Paul**
After captivity	**Letter of James**
Psalms	**Letters of Peter**
Proverbs and Ecclesiastes	**Pastoral Epistles**
Major prophets	**Hebrews**
Minor prophets	Revelation

Missing books

Why is it not in Isaiah and Ezekiel?

Added books

Why is it in Daniel and Revelation?

What meaning is there in the Old and New Testament

The beast will exercise authority over man and it will antagonise God.

How many verses in the Old Testament	How many verses in the New Testament
Seven.	Forty-five.

530 BC
Daniel ch.7 v4-7

AD 96
Revelation ch.11 v7-8; ch.13 v1-8; ch.14 v9-11; ch.16 v2; ch.19 v19-21

Birthday

Most popular Old Testament Exodus.	Most popular New Testament Matthew and Mark.
If the book is missing, it would be **bold** Pentateuch **Joshua and Judges** **History books** **After captivity** **Psalms** **Proverbs and Ecclesiastes** **Major prophets** **Minor prophets**	Gospels **Acts** **Letters of Paul** **Letter of James** **Letters of Peter** **Pastoral Epistles** **Hebrews** **Revelation**
Missing books Why is it not in the Major Prophets.	
Added books In the New Testament, why is it only in the Gospels?	
What meaning is there in the Old and New Testament Birthday means a great feasting for all the people.	
How many verses in the Old Testament Three.	How many verses in the New Testament Two.

1680 BC
Genesis ch.40 v20

1280 BC
Exodus ch.30 v14-15; ch.38 v26-27

AD 30
Matthew ch.14 v6-8
Mark ch.6 v21-22

Blasphemy

Most popular Old Testament	Most popular New Testament
None.	Matthew.

If the book is missing, it would be **bold**	
Pentateuch **Joshua and Judges** **History books** **After captivity** **Psalms** **Proverbs and Ecclesiastes** **Major prophets** **Minor prophets**	Gospels **Acts** **Letters of Paul** **Letter of James** Letters of Peter **Pastoral Epistles** **Hebrews** Revelation

Missing books   Why is it not in the Old Testament?

Added books   Why is it in Matthew's Gospel?

What meaning is there in the Old and New Testament   Jesus was accused of blasphemy for claiming that he was God.

How many verses in the Old Testament	How many verses in the New Testament
None.	Fifteen.

AD 30
Matthew ch.9 v3; ch.12 v31-32; ch.26 v65-67
Luke ch.5 v21
John ch.10 v36-38

AD 80
2 Peter ch.2 v11
Jude ch.1 v9

AD 96
Revelation ch.2 v9; ch.13 v6-7

Body

Most popular Old Testament	Most popular New Testament
Numbers.	1 Corinthians.
If the book is missing, it would be **bold** Pentateuch Joshua and Judges History books After captivity Psalms Proverbs and Ecclesiastes Major prophets Minor prophets	Gospels Acts Letters of Paul Letter of James Letters of Peter Pastoral Epistles Hebrews **Revelation**
Missing books Why is it not in Revelation?	
Added books Why is it in Numbers?	
What meaning is there in the Old and New Testament The body is what makes us as people.	
How many verses in the Old Testament One hundred and Four.	How many verses in the New Testament One hundred and Fifty-four.

1680 BC
Genesis ch.50 v26

1240 BC
Leviticus ch.17 v11; ch.21 v11
Numbers ch.19 v11-12
Deuteronomy ch.21 v22-23; ch.31 v9-10

1060 BC
Judges ch.19 v29

1000 BC
Psalm ch.139 v13

975 BC
2 Samuel ch.18 v17

950 BC
Ecclesiastes ch.11 v10

580 BC
2 Kings ch.13 v21

530 BC
Daniel ch.10 v6

AD 30
Matthew ch.10 v28
Luke ch.12 v23-24

AD 49
1 Thessalonians ch.4 v4-6

AD 53
1 Corinthians ch.6 v19-20; ch.15 v38

AD 55
Romans ch.6 v13-14; ch.8 v10-11
2 Corinthians ch.5 v9-10

AD 61
Ephesians ch.4 v12-13; ch.6 v14-15

AD 64
1 Peter ch.2 v24

Bones

Most popular Old Testament	Most popular New Testament
Ezekiel.	Matthew, John and Hebrews.

If the book is missing, it would be **bold**	
	Gospels
Pentateuch	**Acts**
Joshua and Judges	**Letters of Paul**
History books	**Letter of James**
After captivity	**Letters of Peter**
Psalms	**Pastoral Epistles**
Proverbs and Ecclesiastes	Hebrews
Major prophets	**Revelation**
Minor prophets	

Missing books

Why is it not in Deuteronomy?

Added books

Why is it in Hebrews?

What meaning is there in the Old and New Testament

Bones it means the body of a loved one.

How many verses in the Old Testament	How many verses in the New Testament
Seventy-five.	Three.

1680 BC
Genesis ch.50 v25-26

1300 BC
Job ch.30 v30

1280 BC
Exodus ch.12 v46-47

1010 BC
1 Samuel ch.31 v13

1000 BC
Psalm ch.6 v2; ch.22 v17; ch.53 v5; ch.102 v4

975 BC
2 Samuel ch.21 v14

950 BC
Proverbs ch.12 v4; ch.25 v15

850 BC
1 Kings ch.13 v31-32

690 BC
Micah ch.3 v3

620 BC
Habakkuk ch.3 v13

580 BC
2 Kings ch.13 v21; ch.23 v16
2 Chronicles ch.34 v5
Jeremiah ch.8 v2-3; ch.23 v9
Lamentations ch.3 v4

570 BC
Ezekiel ch.32 v5; ch.37 v2-3

AD 30
Matthew ch.23 v27-28
John ch.19 v36-37

Branch

Most popular Old Testament	Most popular New Testament
Isaiah.	John.
If the book is missing, it would be **bold** Pentateuch **Joshua and Judges** History books After captivity **Psalms** Proverbs and Ecclesiastes Major prophets Minor prophets	Gospels **Acts** Letters of Paul **Letter of James** **Letters of Peter** **Pastoral Epistles** **Hebrews** **Revelation**

Missing books
Why is it not in Psalms?

Added books
Why is it in Isaiah?

What meaning is there in the Old and New Testament
The branch implies a new direction.

How many verses in the Old Testament	How many verses in the New Testament
Twenty-six.	Six.

1680 BC
Genesis ch.2 v11-14

1240 BC
Leviticus ch.14 v4-5
Numbers ch.13 v23-24

1010 BC
1 Samuel ch.2 v30

950 BC
Proverbs ch.26 v9

685 BC
Isaiah ch.4 v2; ch.9 v14; ch.11 v1

580 BC
Jeremiah ch.1 v11

570 BC
Ezekiel ch.17 v4

530 BC
Daniel ch.1 v4

515 BC
Zechariah ch.3 v8-9

AD 30
John ch.15 v2-3; ch.19 v29-30

AD 55
Romans ch.11 v18, v24

Brook

Most popular Old Testament 1 Kings.	Most popular New Testament None.
If the book is missing, it would be **bold** Pentateuch Joshua and Judges History books **After captivity** **Psalms** Proverbs and Ecclesiastes Major prophets **Minor prophets**	**Gospels** **Acts** **Letters of Paul** **Letter of James** **Letters of Peter** **Pastoral Epistles** **Hebrews** **Revelation**
Missing books Why is it not in Psalms?	
Added books Why is it in 1 Kings?	
What meaning is there in the Old and New Testament A brook is like a stream or river.	
How many verses in the Old Testament Twenty-two.	How many verses in the New Testament None.

1300 BC
Job ch.6 v15-17

1240 BC
Deuteronomy ch.2 v14-15

1220 BC
Joshua ch.15 v4

1010 BC
1 Samuel ch.30 v9-10

950 BC
Proverbs ch.18 v4

850 BC
1 Kings ch.17 v3-4

580 BC
2 Chronicles ch.32 v4
Jeremiah ch.15 v18

Captain

Most popular Old Testament	Most popular New Testament
Jeremiah.	Acts.

If the book is missing, it would be bold	
	Gospels
Pentateuch	Acts
Joshua and Judges	**Letters of Paul**
History books	**Letter of James**
After captivity	**Letters of Peter**
Psalms	**Pastoral Epistles**
Proverbs and Ecclesiastes	**Hebrews**
Major prophets	**Revelation**
Minor prophets	

Missing books
Why is it not in Isaiah?

Added books
Why is it in Acts?

What meaning is there in the Old and New Testament
The captain is the appointed leader of the people.

How many verses in the Old Testament	How many verses in the New Testament
Forty-two.	Six.

1680 BC
Genesis ch.37 v36

1010 BC
1 Samuel ch.17 v19; ch.22 v2

975 BC
2 Samuel ch.8 v18

850 BC
2 Kings ch.1 v9

750 BC
Jonah ch.1 v5-6

850 BC
2 Kings ch.25 v20-21
Jeremiah ch.40 v5-6

AD 63
Acts ch.4 v1-2; ch.5 v26-27; ch.10 v1-2; ch.27 v1-2

Cave

Most popular Old Testament Genesis.	Most popular New Testament John.
If the book is missing, it would be **bold** Pentateuch Joshua and Judges History books **After captivity** Psalms **Proverbs and Ecclesiastes** **Major prophets** **Minor prophets**	Gospels **Acts** **Letters of Paul** **Letter of James** **Letters of Peter** **Pastoral Epistles** **Hebrews** **Revelation**
Missing books Why is it not in the Major and Minor Prophets?	
Added books Why is it in Genesis?	
What meaning is there in the Old and New Testament People can go to a cave in the rocks to live there.	
How many verses in the Old Testament Thirty-four.	How many verses in the New Testament One.

1680 BC
Genesis ch.19 v30-31; ch.49 v30-31

1220 BC
Joshua ch.10 v16-17

1060 BC
Judges ch.15 v8

1010 BC
1 Samuel ch.17 v9; ch.22 v1

975 BC
2 Samuel ch.17 v9; ch.23 v13

850 BC
1 Kings ch.18 v4; ch.19 v13

AD 30
John ch.11 v38-39

Chariot

Most popular Old Testament	Most popular New Testament
1 Kings.	None.

If the book is missing, it would be **bold**	
Pentateuch	**Gospels**
Joshua and Judges	**Acts**
History books	**Letters of Paul**
After captivity	**Letter of James**
Psalms	**Letters of Peter**
Proverbs and Ecclesiastes	**Pastoral Epistles**
Major prophets	**Hebrews**
Minor prophets	**Revelation**

Missing books
Why is it not in Proverbs?

Added books
Why is it in 1 Kings?

What meaning is there in the Old and New Testament
The chariot is used as a mark of royalty, above the foot soldiers.

How many verses in the Old Testament	How many verses in the New Testament
Sixty-one.	None.

1680 BC
Genesis ch.41 v43; ch.46 v29

1280 BC
Exodus ch.14 v6-7

1060 BC
Judges ch.4 v15-16

1000 BC
Psalm ch.104 v3

975 BC
2 Samuel ch.15 v1-2
1 Chronicles ch.28 v18-19

950 BC
Song of Songs ch.6 v12

850 BC
1 Kings ch.4 v26; ch.12 v18-19; ch.22 v31-32

580 BC
2 Kings ch.2 v11-12; ch.23 v20

570 BC
Ezekiel ch.23 v23-24

515 BC
Zechariah ch.6 v6

Christian

Most popular Old Testament	Most popular New Testament
None.	1 Corinthians.

If the book is missing, it would be **bold**	
Pentateuch	**Gospels**
Joshua and Judges	Acts
History books	Letters of Paul
After captivity	**Letter of James**
Psalms	Letters of Peter
Proverbs and Ecclesiastes	**Pastoral Epistles**
Major prophets	**Hebrews**
Minor prophets	**Revelation**

Missing books
Why is it not in the Gospels?

Added books
Why is it in 1 Corinthians?

What meaning is there in the Old and New Testament
The word Christian means not doing anything wrong.

How many verses in the Old Testament	How many verses in the New Testament
None.	Twenty-eight.

AD 49
1 Thessalonians ch.4 v6

AD 53
1 Corinthians ch.3 v1; ch.7 v14-15; ch.9 v5-6

AD 54
Galatians ch.3 v3-4

AD 63
Acts ch.26 v28

AD 64
1 Peter ch.3 v15-16; ch.4 v14; ch.5 v9

AD 93
1 John ch.2 v9-10; ch.3 v14; ch.4 v21; ch.5 v16

Church

Most popular Old Testament	Most popular New Testament
None.	Acts.

If the book is missing, it would be **bold**	
	Gospels
Pentateuch	Acts
Joshua and Judges	Letters of Paul
History books	Letter of James
After captivity	Letters of Peter
Psalms	Pastoral Epistles
Proverbs and Ecclesiastes	**Hebrews**
Major prophets	Revelation
Minor prophets	

Missing books
Why is it not in Hebrews?

Added books
Why is it in Acts?

What meaning is there in the Old and New Testament
The strength of the church is to build up all its members.

How many verses in the Old Testament	How many verses in the New Testament
None.	One hundred and Twenty-one.

AD 30
Matthew ch.16 v18; ch.18 v17

AD 53
1 Corinthians ch.1 v10-11; ch.5 v4-5; ch.8 v1-2; ch.12 v28; ch.14 v34-35
Philippians ch.4 v15-16

AD 54
Galatians ch.2 v2

AD 55
Romans ch.14 v19

AD 61
Ephesians ch.1 v23

AD 63
Acts ch.8 v1-2; ch.9 v31; ch.12 v1-2, v5; ch.14 v23-24; ch.20 v28-29

AD 64
1 Timothy ch.3 v5; ch.4 v14-15; ch.5 v20

AD 66
James ch.3 v1-2; ch.5 v14-15

Compassion

Most popular Old Testament	Most popular New Testament
Psalm.	Luke.

If the book is missing, it would be **bold**	
	Gospels
Pentateuch	**Acts**
Joshua and Judges	Letters of Paul
History books	**Letter of James**
After captivity	**Letters of Peter**
Psalms	**Pastoral Epistles**
Proverbs and Ecclesiastes	**Hebrews**
Major prophets	**Revelation**
Minor prophets	

Missing books
Why is it not in Genesis?

Added books
Why is it in Luke's Gospel?

What meaning is there in the Old and New Testament
The Lord has compassion for his people.

How many verses in the Old Testament	How many verses in the New Testament
Thirty.	Ten.

1280 BC
Exodus ch.33 v19-20

1240 BC
Deuteronomy ch.13 v17

1000 BC
Psalm ch.25 v6; ch.51 v1; ch.86 v15; ch.145 v9

720 BC
Hosea ch.2 v19; ch.11 v8

685 BC
Isaiah ch.13 v18; ch.30 v18; ch.54 v7-8

580 BC
2 Chronicles ch.36 v15-16
Jeremiah ch.12 v15-16; ch.13 v14

515 BC
Zechariah ch.10 v6

400 BC
Nehemiah ch.13 v22

AD 30
Matthew ch.14 v14
Mark ch.1 v41-42
Luke ch.7 v13-14; ch.15 v20

AD 53
Philippians ch.1 v8

AD 55
Romans ch.9 v14-15

AD 93
1 John ch.3 v17

Conscience

Most popular Old Testament	Most popular New Testament
1 Samuel.	1 Corinthians.

If the book is missing, it would be **bold**	
Pentateuch	**Gospels** Acts
Joshua and Judges	Letters of Paul
History books	**Letter of James**
After captivity	Letters of Peter
Psalms	Pastoral Epistles
Proverbs and Ecclesiastes	Hebrews
Major prophets	**Revelation**
Minor prophets	

Missing books

Why is it not in the Gospels?

Added books

Why is it in the Pastoral Epistles?

What meaning is there in the Old and New Testament

It speaks about keeping your conscience clear.

How many verses in the Old Testament	How many verses in the New Testament
Six.	Twenty-one.

1680 BC
Genesis ch.37 v26-27

1300 BC
Job ch.27 v6

1010 BC
1 Samuel ch.24 v5; ch.25 v31

975 BC
2 Samuel ch.24 v10

950 BC
Proverbs ch.28 v17

AD 53
1 Corinthians ch.4 v4; ch.8 v9-10

AD 55
Romans ch.2 v15-16; ch.9 v1-2; ch.13 v5; ch.14 v2-4
2 Corinthians ch.1 v12

AD 63
Acts ch.23 v1; ch.24 v16

AD 64
1 Timothy ch.1 v5-6, v19-20; ch.3 v9-10
2 Timothy ch.1 v3
1 Peter ch.3 v16, v21

AD 66
Hebrews ch.13 v18-19

Corruption

Most popular Old Testament	Most popular New Testament
Ezekiel.	2 Peter.

If the book is missing, it would be **bold**	
Pentateuch	Gospels
Joshua and Judges	**Acts**
History books	**Letters of Paul**
After captivity	**Letter of James**
Psalms	Letters of Peter
Proverbs and Ecclesiastes	**Pastoral Epistles**
Major prophets	**Hebrews**
Minor prophets	**Revelation**

Missing book
Why is it not in Psalms?

Added books
Why is it in 2 Peter?

What meaning is there in the Old and New Testament
All mankind is corrupt and based in sin.

How many verses in the Old Testament	How many verses in the New Testament
Fifteen.	Three.

1680 BC
Genesis ch.6 v12-13

950 BC
Proverbs ch.8 v13; ch.28 v16

690 BC
Micah ch.3 v10

685 BC
Isaiah ch.59 v3

620 BC
Habakkuk ch.2 v12

580 BC
2 Kings ch.23 v13-14
Jeremiah ch.6 v28-29

570 BC
Ezekiel ch.16 v47-49; ch.24 v6, v11-13

450 BC
Ezra ch.9 v11-12

AD 30
Luke ch.11 v14

AD 80
2 Peter ch.1 v4; ch.2 v19-20

Council

Most popular Old Testament	Most popular New Testament
Ezra.	Acts.

If the book is missing, it would be **bold**	
	Gospels
Pentateuch	Acts
Joshua and Judges	**Letters of Paul**
History books	**Letter of James**
After captivity	**Letters of Peter**
Psalms	**Pastoral Epistles**
Proverbs and Ecclesiastes	**Hebrews**
Major prophets	**Revelation**
Minor prophets	

Missing books

Why is it not in the Letters of Paul, James and Peter?

Added books

Why is it in Ezra?

What meaning is there in the Old and New Testament

It is a group of men set up by the authorities to lead the rest of mankind.

How many verses in the Old Testament	How many verses in the New Testament
Five.	Thirty-two.

1680 BC
Genesis ch.34 v24-25

1300 BC
Job ch.15 v8

450 BC
Ezra ch.7 v14-15; ch.8 v25-26

AD 30
Matthew ch.26 v59-60
Mark ch.15 v43-44
Luke ch.22 v66-67

AD 63
Acts ch.4 v5-6, v15; ch.5 v22-23, v41; ch.17 v6, v19-20; ch.22 v5; ch.23 v7-9, v15

Crime

Most popular Old Testament	Most popular New Testament
Deuteronomy.	Acts.
If the book is missing, it would be **bold** Pentateuch Joshua and Judges History books **After captivity** **Psalms** Proverbs and Ecclesiastes Major prophets Minor prophets	Gospels Acts **Letters of Paul** **Letter of James** **Letters of Peter** **Pastoral Epistles** **Hebrews** **Revelation**

Missing books
Why is it not in Psalms?

Added books
Why is it in Acts?

What meaning is there in the Old and New Testament
A crime must be punished for it is a shameful thing.

How many verses in the Old Testament	How many verses in the New Testament
Nineteen.	Nine.

1680 BC
Genesis ch.20 v9-10

1300 BC
Job ch.31 v11

1240 BC
Deuteronomy ch.19 v15-18; ch.21 v2-3, v22-23; ch.22 v12; ch.25 v2-3

1060 BC
Judges ch.19 v30

975 BC
2 Samuel ch.3 v28-29
Ecclesiastes ch.8 v11-12

625 BC
Zephaniah ch.3 v1

580 BC
Jeremiah ch.37 v18-19

AD 30
Mark ch.15 v14
Luke ch.11 v48-49

AD 63
Acts ch.18 v14-15; ch.22 v24-25; ch.24 v20-21; ch.25 v8

Dance

Most popular Old Testament	Most popular New Testament
Isaiah and Jeremiah.	Matthew.
If the book is missing, it would be **bold** **Pentateuch** **Joshua and Judges** **History books** **After captivity** **Psalms** Proverbs and Ecclesiastes Major prophets **Minor prophets**	Gospels **Acts** **Letters of Paul** **Letter of James** **Letters of Peter** **Pastoral Epistles** **Hebrews** **Revelation**

Missing books   Why is it not in the History Books?
Added books   Why is it only in the Gospels?
What meaning is there in the Old and New Testament   Dance is like singing and skipping.

How many verses in the Old Testament	How many verses in the New Testament
Seven.	Four.

1300 BC
Job ch.21 v11

950 BC
Ecclesiastes ch.3 v4

685 BC
Isaiah ch.13 v21; ch.22 v13

580 BC
Jeremiah ch.31 v4, v13
Lamentations ch.5 v14

AD 30
Matthew ch.11 v17; ch.14 v6-8

Debt

Most popular Old Testament	Most popular New Testament
Proverbs.	Matthew.

If the book is missing, it would be **bold**	
	Gospels
Pentateuch	**Acts**
Joshua and Judges	Letters of Paul
History books	**Letter of James**
After captivity	**Letters of Peter**
Psalms	**Pastoral Epistles**
Proverbs and Ecclesiastes	**Hebrews**
Major prophets	**Revelation**
Minor prophets	

Missing books
Why is it not in the Major and Minor Prophets?

Added books
Why is it in Proverbs?

What meaning is there in the Old and New Testament
It's poor judgement if you agree to put up a stranger's debt.

How many verses in the Old Testament	How many verses in the New Testament
Eleven.	Seven.

1240 BC
Deuteronomy ch.15 v3; ch.24 v17-18

1010 BC
1 Samuel ch.22 v2

950 BC
Proverbs ch.6 v1-2; ch.11 v15; ch.17 v18; ch.20 v16; ch.22 v26-27

AD 30
Matthew ch.18 v25
Luke ch.7 v43

AD 55
Romans ch.15 v27

Deceit

Most popular Old Testament	Most popular New Testament
Proverbs.	Mark, Acts, 1 Thessalonians and 1 Peter.
If the book is missing, it would be **bold** Pentateuch **Joshua and Judges** History books **After captivity** **Psalms** Proverbs and Ecclesiastes Major prophets Minor prophets	Gospels Acts Letters of Paul **Letter of James** Letters of Peter **Pastoral Epistles** **Hebrews** **Revelation**
Missing books Why is it not in the Psalms?	
Added books Why is it in Numbers?	
What meaning is there in the Old and New Testament Deceit is what the wicked do, but not the Christian.	
How many verses in the Old Testament Nine.	How many verses in the New Testament Four.

1300 BC
Job ch.15 v35

1240 BC
Numbers ch.25 v16-18

1010 BC
1 Samuel ch.17 v18

950 BC
Proverbs ch.6 v12-13; ch.12 v20

720 BC
Hosea ch.11 v12

685 BC
Isaiah ch.24 v16

625 BC
Zephaniah ch.1 v9

580 BC
Jeremiah ch.23 v26-27

AD 30
Mark ch.7 v20-23

AD 49
1 Thessalonians ch.2 v3

AD 63
Acts ch.13 v10-11

AD 64
1 Peter ch.2 v1-2

Demon

Most popular Old Testament	Most popular New Testament
None.	Luke and John.

If the book is missing, it would be **bold**	
	Gospels
Pentateuch	Acts
Joshua and Judges	**Letters of Paul**
History books	**Letter of James**
After captivity	**Letters of Peter**
Psalms	**Pastoral Epistles**
Proverbs and Ecclesiastes	**Hebrews**
Major prophets	**Revelation**
Minor prophets	

Missing books
Why is it not in the Old Testament?

Added books
Why is it only in the Gospels (apart from the one verse in Acts).

What meaning is there in the Old and New Testament
A demon is caused by possession of an evil spirit.

How many verses in the Old Testament	How many verses in the New Testament
None.	Twenty-four.

AD 30
Matthew ch.9 v33; ch.11 v18-19; ch.15 v22; ch.17 v18
Mark ch.5 v18-19; ch.7 v25-26, v30
Luke ch.4 v35
John ch.8 v49, v52; ch.10 v20-21

AD 63
Acts ch.16 v18

Devil

Most popular Old Testament	Most popular New Testament
None.	Matthew and Luke.

If the book is missing, it would be **bold**	
	Gospels
Pentateuch	Acts
Joshua and Judges	Letters of Paul
History books	Letter of James
After captivity	Letters of Peter
Psalms	Pastoral Epistles
Proverbs and Ecclesiastes	Hebrews
Major prophets	Revelation
Minor prophets	

Missing books
Why is it not in Mark's Gospel?

Added books
Why is it in Ephesians?

What meaning is there in the Old and New Testament
Satan and his fallen angels will be going to the lake of fire.

How many verses in the Old Testament	How many verses in the New Testament
None.	Thirty-nine.

AD 30
Matthew ch.4 v1-2; ch.13 v39; ch.25 v41
Luke ch.4 v13; ch.8 v12-13
John ch.6 v70; ch.8 v44; ch.13 v2-3

AD 55
2 Corinthians ch.6 v15-16

AD 61
Ephesians ch.2 v2; ch.6 v11-12

AD 63
Acts ch.10 v38; ch.13 v10-11

AD 64
1 Timothy ch.3 v6
1 Peter ch.5 v8-9

AD 66
Hebrews ch.2 v14-15
James ch.4 v7-8

AD 80
Jude ch.1 v9

AD 93
1 John ch.3 v8-9

AD 96
Revelation ch.2 v10; ch.12 v9, v12; ch.20 v2-3, v10

Disciple

Most popular Old Testament	Most popular New Testament
None.	John.

If the book is missing, it would be **bold**	
	Gospels
Pentateuch	Acts
Joshua and Judges	**Letters of Paul**
History books	**Letter of James**
After captivity	**Letters of Peter**
Psalms	**Pastoral Epistles**
Proverbs and Ecclesiastes	**Hebrews**
Major prophets	**Revelation**
Minor prophets	

Missing books

Why is it not in the Letters of Paul, James and Peter?

Added books

Why is it in John's Gospel?

What meaning is there in the Old and New Testament

The word disciple only occurs during Jesus' ministry.

How many verses in the Old Testament	How many verses in the New Testament
None.	Thirty.

AD 30
Matthew ch.9 v9; ch.13 v52
Luke ch.14 v26-27, v33
John ch.9 v28-29; ch.12 v4-6, v26; ch.13 v23-25; ch.14 v22; ch.18 v15-16; ch.19 v26-27, v38; ch.20 v2-3; ch.21 v7-8, v23

AD 63
Acts ch.16 v1-2

Disease

Most popular Old Testament	Most popular New Testament
Leviticus.	Matthew.

If the book is missing, it would be **bold**	
	Gospels
Pentateuch	**Acts**
Joshua and Judges	**Letters of Paul**
History books	**Letter of James**
After captivity	**Letters of Peter**
Psalms	**Pastoral Epistles**
Proverbs and Ecclesiastes	**Hebrews**
Major prophets	Revelation
Minor prophets	

Missing books
Why is it not in Mark or Luke's Gospels?

Added books
Why is it in Leviticus?

What meaning is there in the Old and New Testament
A disease was to separate the people from illness.

How many verses in the Old Testament	How many verses in the New Testament
Seventy-two.	Five.

1300 BC
Job ch.18 v13-14

1280 BC
Exodus ch.4 v6

1240 BC
Leviticus ch.13 v2, v11, v20-21; v27-28; v42-43, v46; ch.14 v1-3
Numbers ch.5 v1-3
Deuteronomy ch.32 v24

1000 BC
Psalm ch.38 v11; ch.91 v6-7

950 BC
Proverbs ch.5 v11

850 BC
1 Kings ch.8 v37-39

685 BC
Isaiah ch.22 v2-3

580 BC
2 Chronicles ch.16 v12-13; ch.21 v18-19
Jeremiah ch.14 v11-12; ch.27 v8; ch.29 v18-19; ch.38 v2

570 BC
Ezekiel ch.5 v17; ch.6 v11-13; ch.7 v15

445 BC
Malachi ch.3 v11

AD 30
Matthew ch.4 v23-24; ch.9 v35-36; ch.10 v1-2

Dream

Most popular Old Testament Daniel.	Most popular New Testament Matthew.
If the book is missing, it would be **bold** Pentateuch Joshua and Judges History books After captivity Psalms Proverbs and Ecclesiastes Major prophets Minor prophets	Gospels Acts **Letters of Paul** **Letter of James** **Letters of Peter** **Pastoral Epistles** **Hebrews** **Revelation**

Missing books Why is it not in Hebrews?
Added books Why is it in Genesis?
What meaning is there in the Old and New Testament It is a message that we had from God in the night-time.

How many verses in the Old Testament Seventy-nine.	How many verses in the New Testament Six.

1680 BC
Genesis ch.20 v3; ch.31 v10-11, v24; ch.37 v5-6; ch.40 v5-6; ch.41 v7, v15

1300 BC
Job ch.20 v8

1240 BC
Deuteronomy ch.13 v1-2

1060 BC
Judges ch.7 v13

950 BC
Proverbs ch.13 v12

850 BC
1 Kings ch.3 v5, v15

685 BC
Isaiah ch.29 v7

580 BC
Jeremiah ch.23 v25-26

550 BC
Joel ch.2 v28

530 BC
Daniel ch.2 v2-3; v30; ch.4 v5-7, v19; ch.7 v1

AD 30
Matthew ch.1 v20; ch.2 v12, v19-20

Earnest

Most popular Old Testament	Most popular New Testament
1 Kings, 2 Chronicles and Jonah.	James and 1 Peter.

If the book is missing, it would be **bold**	
	Gospels
Pentateuch	**Acts**
Joshua and Judges	**Letters of Paul**
History books	Letter of James
After captivity	Letters of Peter
Psalms	**Pastoral Epistles**
Proverbs and Ecclesiastes	**Hebrews**
Major prophets	**Revelation**
Minor prophets	

Missing books

Why is it not in the Pentateuch?

Added books

Why is it in James?

What meaning is there in the Old and New Testament

The earnest prayer of a righteous man has great power.

How many verses in the Old Testament	How many verses in the New Testament
Three.	Two.

850 BC
1 Kings ch.8 v30

750 BC
Jonah ch.2 v7

AD 64
1 Peter ch.4 v7-8

AD 66
James ch.5 v16-17

Eden

Most popular Old Testament	Most popular New Testament
Ezekiel.	None.

If the book is missing, it would be **bold**	
	Gospels
Pentateuch	**Acts**
Joshua and Judges	**Letters of Paul**
History books	**Letter of James**
After captivity	**Letters of Peter**
Psalms	**Pastoral Epistles**
Proverbs and Ecclesiastes	**Hebrews**
Major prophets	**Revelation**
Minor prophets	

Missing books
Why is it not in the Psalms?

Added books
Why is it in Ezekiel?

What meaning is there in the Old and New Testament
God created a wonderful place called the Garden of Eden.

How many verses in the Old Testament	How many verses in the New Testament
Nineteen.	None.

1680 BC
Genesis ch.2 v8-9; v15-16; ch.3 v23-24; ch.4 v16-17

685 BC
Isaiah ch.51 v3

580 BC
2 Kings ch.19 v12-13

570 BC
Ezekiel ch.28 v13; ch.31 v9, v18; ch.36 v35-36

550 BC
Joel ch.2 v3

Elder

Most popular Old Testament	Most popular New Testament
None.	1 Timothy.

If the book is missing, it would be **bold**	
	Gospels
Pentateuch	**Acts**
Joshua and Judges	Letters of Paul
History books	**Letter of James**
After captivity	Letters of Peter
Psalms	Pastoral Epistles
Proverbs and Ecclesiastes	**Hebrews**
Major prophets	**Revelation**
Minor prophets	

Missing books
Why is it not in the Old Testament?

Added books
Why is it in the Pastoral Epistles?

What meaning is there in the Old and New Testament
An elder must be a man whose life is above reproach.

How many verses in the Old Testament	How many verses in the New Testament
None.	Ten.

AD 64
1 Timothy ch.3 v1-7; ch.5 v19-20
Titus ch.1 v6-9
1 Peter ch.5 v1-3

Exile

Most popular Old Testament	Most popular New Testament
Jeremiah and Ezekiel.	Matthew.

If the book is missing, it would be **bold**	
	Gospels
Pentateuch	Acts
Joshua and Judges	**Letters of Paul**
History books	**Letter of James**
After captivity	**Letters of Peter**
Psalms	**Pastoral Epistles**
Proverbs and Ecclesiastes	**Hebrews**
Major prophets	**Revelation**
Minor prophets	

Missing books
Why is it not in the Psalms and Proverbs?

Added books
Why is it in Matthew's Gospel?

What meaning is there in the Old and New Testament
Time and time again, God said the Israelites will go into exile.

How many verses in the Old Testament	How many verses in the New Testament
One hundred and Eleven.	Five.

1240 BC
Leviticus ch.26 v34-35, v44-45; ch.28 v36-37

850 BC
1 Kings ch.8 v47-48

750 BC
Amos ch.5 v27; ch.7 v17; ch.9 v4

720 BC
Hosea ch.1 v11

690 BC
Micah ch.1 v11; ch.2 v13; ch.4 v10

685 BC
Isaiah ch.5 v13; ch.27 v13

580 BC
2 Kings ch.20 v18; ch.24 v20
Jeremiah ch.2 v37; ch.13 v19-20; ch.29 v7, v19
Lamentations ch.2 v14

570 BC
Ezekiel ch.6 v12-13; ch.11 v14-15; ch.20 v41-42; ch.39 v23, v28-29

515 BC
Zechariah ch.7 v5-7

450 BC
Ezra ch.6 v16-17, v21-22

AD 30
Matthew ch.1 v17

Firstborn

Most popular Old Testament	Most popular New Testament
Exodus and Numbers.	Hebrews.

If the book is missing, it would be **bold**	
	Gospels
Pentateuch	**Acts**
Joshua and Judges	Letters of Paul
History books	**Letter of James**
After captivity	**Letters of Peter**
Psalms	**Pastoral Epistles**
Proverbs and Ecclesiastes	Hebrews
Major prophets	**Revelation**
Minor prophets	

Missing books
Why is it not in Isaiah and Jeremiah?

Added books
Why is it in Hebrews?

What meaning is there in the Old and New Testament
The eldest son he has he rights exclusive only to the firstborn.

How many verses in the Old Testament	How many verses in the New Testament
Ninety-three.	Five.

1680 BC
Genesis ch.25 v34; ch.27 v4; ch.29 v26-27; ch.48 v18; ch.49 v3

1280 BC
Exodus ch.4 v22-23; ch.11 v5-6; ch.13 v2
Numbers ch.3 v13, v45-46
Deuteronomy ch.12 v17-18; ch.15 v19-20; ch.21 v15-17

1220 BC
Joshua ch.6 v26

1000 BC
Psalm ch.89 v27

975 BC
1 Chronicles ch.5 v1-2

690 BC
Micah ch.6 v7-8

570 BC
Ezekiel ch.20 v26

515 BC
Zechariah ch.12 v10-11

400 BC
Nehemiah ch.10 v36

AD 55
Romans ch.8 v29-30

AD 66
Hebrews ch.1 v6; ch.12 v23

Fish

Most popular Old Testament	Most popular New Testament
Genesis and Ezekiel.	Matthew.
If the book is missing, it would be **bold** Pentateuch **Joshua and Judges** History books After captivity Psalms Proverbs and Ecclesiastes Major prophets Minor prophets	Gospels **Acts** Letters of Paul Letter of James **Letters of Peter** **Pastoral Epistles** **Hebrews** **Revelation**

Missing books
Why is it not in Acts?

Added books
Why is it in Ezekiel?

What meaning is there in the Old and New Testament
In the Bible, fish are meant to be caught.

How many verses in the Old Testament	How many verses in the New Testament
Thirty-four.	Thirty-five.

1680 BC
Genesis ch.1 v20-21, v26; ch.9 v2-3

1300 BC
Job ch.12 v8

1280 BC
Exodus ch.7 v18

1240 BC
Numbers ch.11 v5-6
Deuteronomy ch.4 v18-19

1000 BC
Psalm ch.8 v8

950 BC
Ecclesiastes ch.19 v12

850 BC
1 Kings ch.4 v33-34

750 BC
Amos ch.4 v2-3
Jonah ch.1 v17

720 BC
Hosea ch.4 v3-4

685 BC
Isaiah ch.50 v2-3

625 BC
Zephaniah ch.1 v3

620 BC
Habbakuk ch.1 v14-15

570 BC
Ezekiel ch.29 v5; ch.38 v20; ch.47 v9-10

400 BC
Nehemiah ch.3 v3-4; ch.13 v16

AD 30
Matthew ch.4 v19-20; ch.7 v10-11; ch.13 v48-49; ch.14 v19; ch.17 v27
Luke ch.5 v4, v6-7; ch.21 v41-43
John ch.21 v9-11

AD 53
1 Corinthians ch.15 v39

Flesh

Most popular Old Testament	Most popular New Testament
Genesis.	John.

If the book is missing, it would be **bold**	
	Gospels
Pentateuch	**Acts**
Joshua and Judges	Letters of Paul
History books	Letter of James
After captivity	**Letters of Peter**
Psalms	**Pastoral Epistles**
Proverbs and Ecclesiastes	Hebrews
Major prophets	Revelation
Minor prophets	

Missing books

Why is it not in Matthew, Mark and Luke's Gospels?

Added books

Why is it in Job?

What meaning is there in the Old and New Testament

Flesh is like the body, but it's a muscular tissue.

How many verses in the Old Testament	How many verses in the New Testament
Forty.	Fourteen.

1680 BC
Genesis ch.2 v23; ch.6 v3; ch.17 v11-12; ch.29 v14; ch.40 v19

1280 BC
Exodus ch.21 v28

1300 BC
Job ch.10 v11; ch.33 v21-22; ch.41 v23-24

1240 BC
Leviticus ch.26 v29-30
Deuteronomy ch.28 v53-54; ch.32 v42

1060 BC
Judges ch.8 v7

1010 BC
1 Samuel ch.17 v44

1000 BC
Psalm ch.79 v2

975 BC
2 Samuel ch.5 v1-2

850 BC
1 Kings ch.19 v21

690 BC
Micah ch.3 v2-3

685 BC
Isaiah ch.31 v3; ch.49 v26; ch.65 v4

580 BC
Lamentations ch.3 v4-6

570 BC
Ezekiel ch.32 v5; ch.39 v17-18

530 BC
Daniel ch.7 v5

515 BC
Zechariah ch.14 v12-13

AD 30
John ch.6 v52

AD 53
1 Corinthians ch.15 v39

AD 55
2 Corinthians ch.12 v7

AD 66
Hebrews ch.2 v14
James ch.5 v3

AD 96
Revelation ch.17 v16-17

Flood

Most popular Old Testament	Most popular New Testament
Genesis.	Matthew and 1 and 2 Peter.

If the book is missing, it would be **bold**	
	Gospels
Pentateuch	Acts
Joshua and Judges	**Letters of Paul**
History books	**Letter of James**
After captivity	Letters of Peter
Psalms	**Pastoral Epistles**
Proverbs and Ecclesiastes	Hebrews
Major prophets	Revelation
Minor prophets	

Missing books
Why is it not in the Letters of Paul?

Added books
Why is it in Genesis?

What meaning is there in the Old and New Testament
Flood means cutting off and starting again.

How many verses in the Old Testament	How many verses in the New Testament
Forty-two.	Nine.

1680 BC
Genesis ch.6 v17-18; ch.9 v11; ch.49 v4

1300 BC
Job ch.12 v15; ch.20 v28

1000 BC
Psalm ch.6 v6; ch.66 v12

975 BC
2 Samuel ch.5 v20-21

950 BC
Proverbs ch.27 v4

750 BC
Amos ch.5 v24

685 BC
Isaiah ch.8 v7; ch.19 v5; ch.28 v2-3, v19; ch.30 v28; ch.59 v19

630 BC
Nahum ch.1 v8

580 BC
Jeremiah ch.47 v2

570 BC
Ezekiel ch.13 v13-14

530 BC
Daniel ch.9 v26-27; ch.11 v40-41

AD 30
Matthew ch.24 v39

AD 64
1 Peter ch.4 v4-6

AD 66
Hebrews ch.11 v7

AD 80
2 Peter ch.3 v6-7

Foot

Most popular Old Testament	Most popular New Testament
Deuteronomy.	Matthew.

If the book is missing, it would be **bold**	
	Gospels
Pentateuch	Acts
Joshua and Judges	Letters of Paul
History books	**Letter of James**
After captivity	**Letters of Peter**
Psalms	**Pastoral Epistles**
Proverbs and Ecclesiastes	**Hebrews**
Major prophets	Revelation
Minor prophets	

Missing books
Why is it not in After Captivity?

Added books
Why is it in Deuteronomy?

What meaning is there in the Old and New Testament
There were numerous references to foot.

How many verses in the Old Testament	How many verses in the New Testament
Sixty-one.	Sixteen.

1680 BC
Genesis ch.41 v43-44

1300 BC
Job ch.39 v15

1280 BC
Exodus ch.21 v23-25; ch.24 v17-18

1240 BC
Leviticus ch.21 v18-21
Deuteronomy ch.2 v5-6; ch.11 v24

1000 BC
Psalm ch.18 v40; ch.91 v12

975 BC
2 Samuel ch.14 v25-26; ch.15 v17-18; ch.21 v20-21; ch.22 v41

950 BC
Proverbs ch.6 v12-13

685 BC
Isaiah ch.1 v6

670 BC
Ezekiel ch.13 v9

580 BC
2 Kings ch.19 v24
2 Chronicles ch.16 v12-13

AD 30
Matthew ch.18 v8-9
Luke ch.14 v9
John ch.20 v12-13

AD 53
1 Corinthians ch.12 v15-16

AD 63
Acts ch.7 v5; ch.20 v18-19

AD 96
Revelation ch.10 v2-3

Garden

Most popular Old Testament	Most popular New Testament
Genesis.	Luke.

If the book is missing, it would be **bold**	
Pentateuch	Gospels
Joshua and Judges	**Acts**
History books	**Letters of Paul**
After captivity	**Letter of James**
Psalms	**Letters of Peter**
Proverbs and Ecclesiastes	**Pastoral Epistles**
Major prophets	**Hebrews**
Minor prophets	**Revelation**

Missing books
Why is it not in Revelation?

Added books
Why is it in the Song of Songs or Psalms?

What meaning is there in the Old and New Testament
God made a delightful garden, but man ruined it.

How many verses in the Old Testament	How many verses in the New Testament
Forty-seven.	Six.

1680 BC
Genesis ch.2 v8-11; ch.3 v8-10, v23-24; ch.13 v10

1300 BC
Job ch.8 v16

1240 BC
Deuteronomy ch.11 v10-11

950 BC
Song of Songs ch.4 v12

850 BC
1 Kings ch.4 v25; ch.21 v2

685 BC
Isaiah ch.1 v30; ch.5 v7; ch.58 v11-12; ch.61 v11 - ch.62 v1

580 BC
2 Kings ch.25 v4
Jeremiah ch.31 v12-13
Lamentations ch.2 v6

570 BC
Ezekiel ch.31 v8; ch.36 v35

550 BC
Joel ch.2 v3

465 BC
Esther ch.1 v5-6

400 BC
Nehemiah ch.3 v15-16

AD 30
Matthew ch.13 v32
Luke ch.13 v6-7

Generation

Most popular Old Testament	Most popular New Testament
Exodus.	Luke.

If the book is missing, it would be **bold**	
	Gospels
Pentateuch	Acts
Joshua and Judges	**Letters of Paul**
History books	**Letter of James**
After captivity	**Letters of Peter**
Psalms	**Pastoral Epistles**
Proverbs and Ecclesiastes	**Hebrews**
Major prophets	**Revelation**
Minor prophets	

Missing books

Why is it not in Paul's Letters?

Added books

Why is in Exodus?

What meaning is there in the Old and New Testament

God made his covenant with the Israelites for generation after generation.

How many verses in the Old Testament	How many verses in the New Testament
One hundred and Nine.	Twenty-three.

1680 BC
Genesis ch.17 v7-8, v12-13

1280 BC
Exodus ch.12 v14-15; ch.17 v16; ch.29 v42; ch.31 v13

1240 BC
Leviticus ch.3 v17; ch.7 v36; ch.23 v43
Numbers ch.18 v23; ch.32 v13-14
Deuteronomy ch.32 v20

1060 BC
Judges ch.2 v10

1000 BC
Psalm ch.78 v7; ch.79 v13; ch.102 v12

685 BC
Isaiah ch.13 v20; ch.51 v8

580 BC
Jeremiah ch.7 v29

550 BC
Joel ch.1 v3

465 BC
Esther ch.9 v28

AD 30
Matthew ch.23 v36; ch.24 v34-35
Luke ch.1 v50; ch.17 v25

AD 63
Acts ch.2 v40

Gentleness

Most popular Old Testament	Most popular New Testament
None.	2 Corinthians, Galatians, Colossians and 1 Timothy.

If the book is missing, it would be **bold**	
Pentateuch	**Gospels**
Joshua and Judges	**Acts**
History books	Letters of Paul
After captivity	**Letter of James**
Psalms	**Letters of Peter**
Proverbs and Ecclesiastes	Pastoral Epistles
Major prophets	**Hebrews**
Minor prophets	**Revelation**

Missing books
Why is it not in the Old Testament?

Added books
Why is it in Galatians?

What meaning is there in the Old and New Testament
The Holy Spirit produces this gentleness in our lives.

How many verses in the Old Testament	How many verses in the New Testament
None.	Four.

AD 54
Galatians ch.5 v22-23

AD 55
2 Corinthians ch.10 v1-2

AD 61
Colossians ch.3 v12-13

AD 64
1 Timothy ch.6 v11-12

Giant

Most popular Old Testament	Most popular New Testament
1 Samuel.	None.

If the book is missing, it would be **bold**	
	Gospels
Pentateuch	**Acts**
Joshua and Judges	**Letters of Paul**
History books	**Letter of James**
After captivity	**Letters of Peter**
Psalms	**Pastoral Epistles**
Proverbs and Ecclesiastes	**Hebrews**
Major prophets	**Revelation**
Minor prophets	

Missing books Why is it not in the New Testament?

Added books Why is it in 1 Samuel?

What meaning is there in the Old and New Testament The giants were big, enormous people.

How many verses in the Old Testament	How many verses in the New Testament
Four.	None.

1680 BC
Genesis ch.6 v4

1240 BC
Deuteronomy ch.3 v11

1010 BC
1 Samuel ch.17 v24-25; ch.19 v5

Glass

Most popular Old Testament	Most popular New Testament
Job.	Revelation.

If the book is missing, it would be **bold**	
	Gospels
Pentateuch	**Acts**
Joshua and Judges	**Letters of Paul**
History books	**Letter of James**
After captivity	**Letters of Peter**
Psalms	**Pastoral Epistles**
Proverbs and Ecclesiastes	**Hebrews**
Major prophets	Revelation
Minor prophets	

Missing books
Why is it not in the Pentateuch?

Added books
Why is it in Revelation?

What meaning is there in the Old and New Testament
The glass was sharp, sparkling like a crystal and was clear.

How many verses in the Old Testament	How many verses in the New Testament
One.	Four.

1300 BC
Job ch.41 v30

AD 96
Revelation ch.4 v6; ch.15 v2; ch.21 v18-19, v21

Godliness

Most popular Old Testament	Most popular New Testament
Proverbs.	1 Timothy.

If the book is missing, it would be **bold**	
	Gospels
Pentateuch	Acts
Joshua and Judges	**Letters of Paul**
History books	**Letter of James**
After captivity	Letters of Peter
Psalms	Pastoral Epistles
Proverbs and Ecclesiastes	**Hebrews**
Major prophets	**Revelation**
Minor prophets	

Missing books
Why is it not in the Gospels?

Added books
Why is it in 1 Timothy?

What meaning is there in the Old and New Testament
Godliness is a virtue, while sin is not.

How many verses in the Old Testament	How many verses in the New Testament
Nine.	Eight.

1000 BC
Psalm ch.132 v9

950 BC
Proverbs ch.11 v6; ch.13 v6; ch.14 v34; ch.15 v9; ch.16 v8

850 BC
1 Kings ch.9 v4-5

685 BC
Isaiah ch.58 v8

AD 63
Acts ch.3 v12-13

AD 64
1 Timothy ch.2 v2-3; ch.4 v8-9; ch.5 v4; ch.6 v5-7

AD 80
2 Peter ch.1 v5-7

Gospel

Most popular Old Testament	Most popular New Testament
None.	Galatians.

If the book is missing, it would be **bold**	
	Gospels
Pentateuch	**Acts**
Joshua and Judges	Letters of Paul
History books	**Letter of James**
After captivity	**Letters of Peter**
Psalms	**Pastoral Epistles**
Proverbs and Ecclesiastes	**Hebrews**
Major prophets	**Revelation**
Minor prophets	

Missing books
Why is it not in Acts?

Added books
Why is it in Galatians?

What meaning is there in the Old and New Testament
Preaching the gospel message.

How many verses in the Old Testament	How many verses in the New Testament
None.	Five.

AD 54
Galatians ch.1 v11-12; ch.2 v5, v7-8, v14

AD 55
2 Corinthians ch.11 v4

Government

Most popular Old Testament	Most popular New Testament
Isaiah.	Luke and Acts.

If the book is missing, it would be **bold**	
Pentateuch **Joshua and Judges** History books After captivity **Psalms** Proverbs and Ecclesiastes Major prophets Minor prophets	Gospels Acts Letters of Paul **Letter of James** **Letters of Peter** Pastoral Epistles **Hebrews** **Revelation**

Missing books

Why is it not in the Pentateuch or Revelation?

Added books

Why is it in Isaiah?

What meaning is there in the Old and New Testament

The government stood for a dignitary who was then responsible.

How many verses in the Old Testament	How many verses in the New Testament
Seven.	Eleven.

950 BC
Proverbs ch.28 v2

850 BC
1 Kings ch.9 v22-23

685 BC
Isaiah ch.9 v6-7; ch.54 v14

530 BC
Daniel ch.6 v4

465 BC
Esther ch.3 v9

AD 30
Mark ch.6 v21-22
Luke ch.3 v13; ch.23 v2, v19-20
John ch.4 v46-47

AD 55
Romans ch.13 v6-7

AD 63
Acts ch.19 v40-41; ch.25 v8; ch.28 v17-18

AD 64
Titus ch.3 v1-2

Governor

Most popular Old Testament	Most popular New Testament
Ezra.	Acts.

If the book is missing, it would be **bold**	
	Gospels
Pentateuch	Acts
Joshua and Judges	Letters of Paul
History books	**Letter of James**
After captivity	**Letters of Peter**
Psalms	**Pastoral Epistles**
Proverbs and Ecclesiastes	**Hebrews**
Major prophets	**Revelation**
Minor prophets	

Missing books
Why is it not in the Pastoral Epistles?

Added books
Why is it in Haggai and Ezra?

What meaning is there in the Old and New Testament
A governor is appointed by the crown to oversee the people.

How many verses in the Old Testament	How many verses in the New Testament
Thirty-nine.	Thirty-four.

1680 BC
Genesis ch.45 v8

950 BC
Proverbs ch.6 v7

850 BC
1 Kings ch.4 v19-20

580 BC
2 Kings ch.23 v8
2 Chronicles ch.34 v8-9
Jeremiah ch.41 v18

515 BC
Haggai ch.2 v21-22

450 BC
Ezra ch.2 v63; ch.5 v14-15

445 BC
Malachi ch.1 v18

400 BC
Nehemiah ch.5 v14

AD 30
Matthew ch.27 v2
Luke ch.2 v2; ch.19 v17

AD 63
Acts ch.13 v7; ch.18 v12-13

Guest

Most popular Old Testament	Most popular New Testament
2 Samuel.	Luke.

If the book is missing, it would be **bold**	
Pentateuch	Gospels
Joshua and Judges	**Acts**
History books	Letters of Paul
After captivity	**Letter of James**
Psalms	**Letters of Peter**
Proverbs and Ecclesiastes	**Pastoral Epistles**
Major prophets	**Hebrews**
Minor prophets	**Revelation**

Missing books

Why is it not in the Major and Minor Prophets?

Added books

Why is it in Luke's Gospel?

What meaning is there in the Old and New Testament

A guest is someone who visits a neighbour's house.

How many verses in the Old Testament	How many verses in the New Testament
Seven.	Six.

1060 BC
Judges ch.19 v23-24

1010 BC
1 Samuel ch.9 v23-24; ch.21 v5

1000 BC
Psalm ch.39 v12

975 BC
2 Samuel ch.12 v4; ch.15 v19-20

AD 30
Luke ch.5 v29-30; ch.19 v7; ch.22 v10-12

AD 61
Philemon ch.1 v22

Hair

Most popular Old Testament	Most popular New Testament
Leviticus.	1 Corinthians.

If the book is missing, it would be **bold**	
Pentateuch	Gospels
Joshua and Judges	Acts
History books	Letters of Paul
After captivity	**Letter of James**
Psalms	**Letters of Peter**
Proverbs and Ecclesiastes	Pastoral Epistles
Major prophets	**Hebrews**
Minor prophets	Revelation

Missing books
Why is it not in Psalms?

Added books
Why is it in Leviticus?

What meaning is there in the Old and New Testament
The hair is important for the people of Israel.

How many verses in the Old Testament	How many verses in the New Testament
Seventy-seven.	Eighteen.

1680 BC
Genesis ch.25 v25

1300 BC
Job ch.4 v15-16; ch.18 v4-5

1280 BC
Exodus ch.35 v23-24

1240 BC
Leviticus ch.14 v8; ch.19 v27
Numbers ch.6 v5-6
Deuteronomy ch.14 v1-3

1060 BC
Judges ch.16 v13

1010 BC
1 Samuel ch.14 v45-46

975 BC
2 Samuel ch.2 v16

950 BC
Proverbs ch.16 v31-32
Song of Songs ch.5 v11-12

685 BC
Isaiah ch.3 v24; ch.46 v4

580 BC
2 Kings ch.9 v30-31

570 BC
Ezekiel ch.8 v3

530 BC
Daniel ch.7 v9

450 BC
Ezra ch.9 v3-4

AD 30
Matthew ch.5 v36-37; ch.6 v17-18
Luke ch.21 v18-19

AD 53
1 Corinthians ch.11 v6, v15-16

AD 64
1 Timothy ch.2 v9-10

AD 96
Revelation ch.1 v14-15

Hail

Most popular Old Testament	Most popular New Testament
Exodus.	John.

If the book is missing, it would be **bold**	
	Gospels
Pentateuch	**Acts**
Joshua and Judges	**Letters of Paul**
History books	**Letter of James**
After captivity	**Letters of Peter**
Psalms	**Pastoral Epistles**
Proverbs and Ecclesiastes	**Hebrews**
Major prophets	Revelation
Minor prophets	

Missing books
Why is it not in Luke's Gospel?

Added books
Why is it in Exodus?

What meaning is there in the Old and New Testament
The Lord manages the rain and hail.

How many verses in the Old Testament	How many verses in the New Testament
Twenty-two.	Six.

1300 BC
Job ch.38 v22-23

1280 BC
Exodus ch.9 v22, v25-26

1220 BC
Joshua ch.10 v11

1000 BC
Psalm ch.18 v12-13; ch.147 v17-18; ch.148 v17

515 BC
Haggai ch.2 v17

AD 96
Revelation ch.8 v7

Hate

Most popular Old Testament Psalms.	Most popular New Testament Luke.
If the book is missing, it would be **bold** Pentateuch Joshua and Judges History books After captivity Psalms Proverbs and Ecclesiastes Major prophets Minor prophets	Gospels **Acts** Letters of Paul **Letter of James** **Letters of Peter** Pastoral Epistles Hebrews Revelation
Missing books Why is it not in Acts?	
Added books Why is it in Proverbs?	
What meaning is there in the Old and New Testament The word hate means active dislike.	
How many verses in the Old Testament Eighty-two.	How many verses in the New Testament Twenty-two.

1680 BC
Genesis ch.26 v27

1300 BC
Job ch.7 v16-17

1240 BC
Leviticus ch.26 v17
Numbers ch.21 v5
Deuteronomy ch.1 v27; ch.30 v7-8

1060 BC
Judges ch.15 v2

1010 BC
1 Samuel ch.27 v12

1000 BC
Psalm ch.5 v5-6; ch.97 v10; ch.119 v85; ch.120 v6

975 BC
2 Samuel ch.19 v6

950 BC
Proverbs ch.8 v13; ch.12 v1
Ecclesiastes ch.2 v17-18

720 BC
Hosea ch.9 v15

690 BC
Micah ch.3 v9

685 BC
Isaiah ch.61 v8

580 BC
2 Chronicles ch.19 v2-3
Jeremiah ch.44 v4-6

445 BC
Malachi ch.2 v16

AD 30
Matthew ch.10 v22; ch.24 v10
Luke ch.6 v22-23
John ch.7 v7

AD 55
Romans ch.1 v29-30; ch.12 v9-10

AD 64
2 Timothy ch.3 v3-4

AD 66
Hebrews ch.1 v9

Health

Most popular Old Testament	Most popular New Testament
Psalms.	None.

If the book is missing, it would be **bold**	
	Gospels
Pentateuch	**Acts**
Joshua and Judges	**Letters of Paul**
History books	**Letter of James**
After captivity	**Letters of Peter**
Psalms	**Pastoral Epistles**
Proverbs and Ecclesiastes	**Hebrews**
Major prophets	**Revelation**
Minor prophets	

Missing books

Why is it not in the New Testament?

Added books

Why is it in Job?

What meaning is there in the Old and New Testament

God gives good health.

How many verses in the Old Testament	How many verses in the New Testament
Thirteen.	None.

1300 BC
Job ch.2 v4-5; ch.21 v24-26

1000 BC
Psalm ch.30 v2; ch.38 v3-8; ch.41 v3; ch.73 v26-27

950 BC
Proverbs ch.15 v30-31
Ecclesiastes ch.5 v19-20

685 BC
Isaiah ch.38 v16-17

580 BC
Jeremiah ch.30 v17
Lamentations ch.4 v7

Hell

Most popular Old Testament	Most popular New Testament
Job.	Matthew.
If the book is missing, it would be **bold**	
Pentateuch **Joshua and Judges** **History books** **After captivity** **Psalms** **Proverbs and Ecclesiastes** **Major prophets** **Minor prophets**	Gospels **Acts** Letters of Paul Letter of James Letters of Peter **Pastoral Epistles** **Hebrews** **Revelation**
Missing books Why is it not in Daniel and Revelation?	
Added books Why is it in Matthew's Gospel?	
What meaning is there in the Old and New Testament The place where hell exists.	
How many verses in the Old Testament	How many verses in the New Testament
One.	Sixteen.

1300 BC
Job ch.31 v12-13

AD 30
Matthew ch.5 v22; ch.7 v13-15; ch.10 v28-29; ch.16 v18-19; ch.23 v15, v33

AD 55
Romans ch.8 v38 - ch.9 v1

AD 66
James ch.3 v5-6

AD 80
2 Peter ch.2 v4-5

Hire

Most popular Old Testament	Most popular New Testament
2 Chronicles.	Matthew and Luke.

If the book is missing, it would be **bold**	
	Gospels
Pentateuch	**Acts**
Joshua and Judges	**Letters of Paul**
History books	**Letter of James**
After captivity	**Letters of Peter**
Psalms	**Pastoral Epistles**
Proverbs and Ecclesiastes	**Hebrews**
Major prophets	**Revelation**
Minor prophets	

Missing books

Why is it not in Jeremiah and Ezekiel?

Added books

Why is it in 2 Chronicles?

What meaning is there in the Old and New Testament

Hire means giving money to agree to give something back.

How many verses in the Old Testament	How many verses in the New Testament
Ten.	Two.

1240 BC
Leviticus ch.25 v50-51

1060 BC
Judges ch.9 v4-5

975 BC
1 Chronicles ch.19 v6-7

580 BC
2 Kings ch.22 v6-7
2 Chronicles ch.25 v6-9

685 BC
Isaiah ch.7 v20; ch.46 v6

515 BC
Zechariah ch.8 v10

AD 30
Matthew ch.20 v1-2
Luke ch.15 v15-16

Holiness

Most popular Old Testament	Most popular New Testament
Ezekiel.	1 and 2 Corinthians.

If the book is missing, it would be **bold**	
	Gospels
Pentateuch	**Acts**
Joshua and Judges	Letters of Paul
History books	**Letter of James**
After captivity	**Letters of Peter**
Psalms	Pastoral Epistles
Proverbs and Ecclesiastes	Hebrews
Major prophets	**Revelation**
Minor prophets	

Missing books
Why is it not in Revelation?

Added books
Why is it in Ezekiel?

What meaning is there in the Old and New Testament
God is manifested through his holiness.

How many verses in the Old Testament	How many verses in the New Testament
Thirty-one.	Nine.

1280 BC
Exodus ch.15 v11; ch.39 v30

1240 BC
Leviticus ch.8 v9; ch.10 v3; ch.22 v32-33
Numbers ch.20 v12-13

1000 BC
Psalm ch.29 v2; ch.89 v35

750 BC
Amos ch.4 v2

685 BC
Isaiah ch.35 v8

570 BC
Ezekiel ch.20 v41-42; ch.38 v23; ch.44 v19

400 BC
Nehemiah ch.13 v22

AD 30
Luke ch.1 v75

AD 49
1 Thessalonians ch.4 v4-6

AD 53
1 Corinthians ch.7 v14-15

AD 55
Romans ch.6 v22-23
2 Corinthians ch.1 v12; ch.7 v1

AD 64
1 Timothy ch.2 v14-15

AD 66
Hebrews ch.12 v10-11

Hook

Most popular Old Testament 2 Kings, Job, Isaiah and Amos.	Most popular New Testament None.
If the book is missing, it would be **bold** **Pentateuch** **Joshua and Judges** History books **After captivity** **Psalms** **Proverbs and Ecclesiastes** Major prophets Minor prophets	**Gospels** **Acts** **Letters of Paul** **Letter of James** **Letters of Peter** **Pastoral Epistles** **Hebrews** **Revelation**

Missing books Why is it not in the New Testament?
Added books Why is it in Amos?
What meaning is there in the Old and New Testament The word hook means you will be led into undesirable spaces.

How many verses in the Old Testament Four.	How many verses in the New Testament None.

1300 BC
Job ch.41 v1-2

750 BC
Amos ch.4 v2-3

685 BC
Isaiah ch.37 v29

580 BC
2 Kings ch.19 v28

Horn

Most popular Old Testament	Most popular New Testament
Daniel.	None.

If the book is missing, it would be **bold**	
	Gospels
Pentateuch	**Acts**
Joshua and Judges	**Letters of Paul**
History books	**Letter of James**
After captivity	**Letters of Peter**
Psalms	**Pastoral Epistles**
Proverbs and Ecclesiastes	**Hebrews**
Major prophets	**Revelation**
Minor prophets	

Missing books
Why is it not in Hebrews?

Added books
Why is it in Daniel?

What meaning is there in the Old and New Testament
The word horn indicates a call to arms.

How many verses in the Old Testament	How many verses in the New Testament
Forty-three.	None.

1300 BC
Job ch.39 v25

1280 BC
Exodus ch.19 v13, v19-20

1240 BC
Leviticus ch.25 v9-10

1220 BC
Joshua ch.6 v4-5

1060 BC
Judges ch.6 v34

1010 BC
1 Samuel ch.13 v3-4

1000 BC
Psalm ch.81 v3-4; ch.150 v3

975 BC
2 Samuel ch.18 v16-17

850 BC
1 Kings ch.1 v34-35, v41

750 BC
Amos ch.2 v2; ch.3 v6

685 BC
Isaiah ch.18 v3

550 BC
Joel ch.2 v15

530 BC
Daniel ch.7 v21-22

515 BC
Zechariah ch.9 v14

Horse

Most popular Old Testament	Most popular New Testament
Esther.	Revelation.

If the book is missing, it would be **bold**	
	Gospels
Pentateuch	**Acts**
Joshua and Judges	**Letters of Paul**
History books	Letter of James
After captivity	**Letters of Peter**
Psalms	**Pastoral Epistles**
Proverbs and Ecclesiastes	**Hebrews**
Major prophets	Revelation
Minor prophets	

Missing books

Why is it not in the Letters of Paul?

Added books

Why is it in Esther?

What meaning is there in the Old and New Testament

The horse was the only thing they could use to get around.

How many verses in the Old Testament	How many verses in the New Testament
Twenty-four.	Nine.

1300 BC
Job ch.39 v18-19

1280 BC
Exodus ch.15 v1

1000 BC
Psalm ch.32 v9; ch.147 v10

950 BC
Proverbs ch.21 v31

580 BC
2 Kings ch.14 v20
2 Chronicles ch.23 v15
Jeremiah ch.8 v6

570 BC
Ezekiel ch.23 v20-21

515 BC
Zechariah ch.12 v4-5

465 BC
Esther ch.6 v9

400 BC
Nehemiah ch.3 v28-29

AD 66
James ch.3 v3-4

AD 96
Revelation ch.6 v4; ch.19 v11-12, v19-20

Hospitality

Most popular Old Testament	Most popular New Testament
None.	Matthew.

If the book is missing, it would be **bold**	
	Gospels
Pentateuch	**Acts**
Joshua and Judges	Letters of Paul
History books	**Letter of James**
After captivity	**Letters of Peter**
Psalms	**Pastoral Epistles**
Proverbs and Ecclesiastes	Hebrews
Major prophets	**Revelation**
Minor prophets	

Missing books
Why is it not in the Old Testament?

Added books
Why is it in Romans?

What meaning is there in the Old and New Testament
Hospitality is to invite people to stay in your house.

How many verses in the Old Testament	How many verses in the New Testament
None.	Four.

AD 30
Matthew ch.10 v10; ch.25 v38-39
Luke ch.10 v7

AD 55
Romans ch.12 v13

AD 66
Hebrews ch.13 v2-3

Host

Most popular Old Testament	Most popular New Testament
None.	Luke.

If the book is missing, it would be **bold**	
Pentateuch	Gospels
Joshua and Judges	**Acts**
History books	Letters of Paul
After captivity	**Letter of James**
Psalms	**Letters of Peter**
Proverbs and Ecclesiastes	**Pastoral Epistles**
Major prophets	**Hebrews**
Minor prophets	**Revelation**

Missing books
Why is it not in the Pentateuch?

Added books
Why is it in Luke's Gospel?

What meaning is there in the Old and New Testament
The word host means proprietor.

How many verses in the Old Testament	How many verses in the New Testament
None.	Eight.

AD 30
Luke ch.2 v13-15; ch.14 v9, v12-13
John ch.2 v10

AD 55
Romans ch.16 v23

AD 66
Hebrews ch.13 v2-3

Hour

Most popular Old Testament Judges, Jeremiah, Daniel and Micah.	Most popular New Testament Matthew.
If the book is missing, it would be **bold** **Pentateuch** Joshua and Judges **History books** After captivity **Psalms** **Proverbs and Ecclesiastes** Major prophets Minor prophets	Gospels Acts Letters of Paul **Letter of James** **Letters of Peter** **Pastoral Epistles** **Hebrews** Revelation

Missing books Why is it not in Isaiah and Ezekiel?
Added books Why is it in Matthew's Gospel?
What meaning is there in the Old and New Testament The word hour means something bad will suddenly come.

How many verses in the Old Testament Four.	How many verses in the New Testament Twenty.

1060 BC
Judges ch.10 v13-15

690 BC
Micah ch.2 v8

580 BC
Jeremiah ch.44 v10

530 BC
Daniel ch.4 v33

AD 30
Matthew ch.8 v13; ch.20 v12; ch.24 v36; ch.25 v13-14; ch.26 v40-41
Luke ch.22 v59-60; ch.24 v33-44
John ch.12 v27-28; ch.13 v1; ch.17 v1-2

AD 63
Acts ch.16 v33
1 Corinthians ch.15 v30-31

AD 93
1 John ch.2 v18-19
Revelation ch.8 v1-2; ch.9 v15-16

Hunting

Most popular Old Testament	Most popular New Testament
1 Samuel.	None.

If the book is missing, it would be **bold**	
	Gospels
Pentateuch	**Acts**
Joshua and Judges	**Letters of Paul**
History books	**Letter of James**
After captivity	**Letters of Peter**
Psalms	**Pastoral Epistles**
Proverbs and Ecclesiastes	**Hebrews**
Major prophets	**Revelation**
Minor prophets	

Missing books
Why is it not in the New Testament?

Added books
Why is it in 1 Samuel?

What meaning is there in the Old and New Testament
Hunting implies battle.

How many verses in the Old Testament	How many verses in the New Testament
Six.	None.

1240 BC
Leviticus ch.17 v13-14

1010 BC
1 Samuel ch.24 v11-12; ch.27 v1-2, v4

685 BC
Isaiah ch.7 v24-25

625 BC
Zephaniah ch.3 v3-4

Husband

Most popular Old Testament	Most popular New Testament
Numbers.	1 Corinthians.

If the book is missing, it would be **bold**	
Pentateuch	Gospels
Joshua and Judges	Acts
History books	Letters of Paul
After captivity	**Letter of James**
Psalms	Letters of Peter
Proverbs and Ecclesiastes	Pastoral Epistles
Major prophets	**Hebrews**
Minor prophets	Revelation

Missing books

Why is it not in Hebrews?

Added books

Why is it in Numbers and 1 Corinthians?

What meaning is there in the Old and New Testament

If you are a man and you get married, then you will be a husband.

How many verses in the Old Testament	How many verses in the New Testament
Eighty-two.	Thirty-three.

1680 BC
Genesis ch.3 v6-7, v16-17

1280 BC
Exodus ch.21 v22-23

1240 BC
Numbers ch.5 v20; ch.30 v11-14
Deuteronomy ch.21 v13-14

1060 BC
Judges ch.13 v10; ch.19 v2-3

1150 BC
Ruth ch.4 v10

1010 BC
1 Samuel ch.25 v19

1000 BC
Psalm ch.45 v11

975 BC
2 Samuel ch.11 v26-27

950 BC
Proverbs ch.2 v17; ch.12 v4-5; ch.31 v11-12

720 BC
Hosea ch.2 v7

685 BC
Isaiah ch.54 v6

580 BC
2 Kings ch.4 v9-10
Jeremiah ch.3 v20

570 BC
Ezekiel ch.16 v45

550 BC
Joel ch.1 v8

AD 30
Mark ch.10 v12
John ch.4 v16-18

AD 53
1 Corinthians ch.7 v2-4, v10-11, v15-16

AD 55
Romans ch.7 v2-3
2 Corinthians ch.11 v2-3

AD 61
Ephesians ch.5 v22-24, v33

AD 64
1 Timothy ch.5 v9-10

AD 96
Revelation ch.21 v2

Idolatry

Most popular Old Testament	Most popular New Testament
Ezekiel.	Romans, 1 Corinthians, Galatians and Revelation.
If the book is missing, it would be **bold** Pentateuch Joshua and Judges History books **After captivity** **Psalms** **Proverbs and Ecclesiastes** Major prophets Minor prophets	**Gospels** **Acts** Letters of Paul **Letter of James** **Letters of Peter** **Pastoral Epistles** Hebrews Revelation
Missing books Why is it not in Isaiah?	
Added books Why is it in Deuteronomy?	
What meaning is there in the Old and New Testament The people followed their gods and it was idolatry.	
How many verses in the Old Testament Sixteen.	How many verses in the New Testament Four.

1280 BC
Exodus ch.23 v32 - ch.24 v1

1240 BC
Numbers ch.31 v2

720 BC
Hosea ch.4 v17

690 BC
Micah ch.1 v5-6

580 BC
2 Kings ch.9 v22

570 BC
Ezekiel ch.14 v4-5; ch.23 v48-49; ch.24 v13

AD 55
Romans ch.2 v22-24

AD 54
Galatians ch.5 v19-21

AD 96
Revelation ch.21 v27

Ignorance

Most popular Old Testament Job.	Most popular New Testament Acts.
If the book is missing, it would be **bold** **Pentateuch** **Joshua and Judges** **History books** **After captivity** **Psalms** **Proverbs and Ecclesiastes** Major prophets **Minor prophets**	**Gospels** Acts Letters of Paul **Letter of James** **Letters of Peter** Pastoral Epistles Hebrews **Revelation**
Missing books Why is it not in the Pentateuch?	
Added books Why is it the Letters of Paul?	
What meaning is there in the Old and New Testament Ignorance equals unawareness.	
How many verses in the Old Testament Five.	How many verses in the New Testament Four.

1300 BC
Job ch.4 v21; ch.34 v35; ch.42 v3-4

685 BC
Isaiah ch.44 v18-19

570 BC
Ezekiel ch.45 v20

AD 63
Acts ch.3 v17-19, v30-31

AD 64
1 Timothy ch.1 v13-14

AD 66
Hebrews ch.9 v7-8

Image

Most popular Old Testament Judges.	Most popular New Testament Acts, 1 & 2 Corinthians, Colossians and James.
If the book is missing, it would be **bold** Pentateuch Joshua and Judges History books **After captivity** Psalms **Proverbs and Ecclesiastes** Major prophets Minor prophets	**Gospels** Acts Letters of Paul Letter of James **Letters of Peter** **Pastoral Epistles** **Hebrews** **Revelation**
Missing books Why is it not in Ezekiel?	
Added books Why is it in Colossians?	
What meaning is there in the Old and New Testament God made man and woman in his image.	
How many verses in the Old Testament Twenty-two.	How many verses in the New Testament Four.

1680 BC
Genesis ch.1 v26; ch.9 v6-7

1280 BC
Exodus ch.20 v4-5

1060 BC
Judges ch.17 v3; ch.18 v20-21

1000 BC
Psalm ch.106 v19

685 BC
Isaiah ch.40 v18; ch.48 v5

620 BC
Habakkuk ch.2 v18

580 BC
2 Kings ch.21 v7
Jeremiah ch.2 v27

AD 63
Acts ch.19 v35-37

AD 53
1 Corinthians ch.11 v7-8

AD 55
2 Corinthians ch.3 v18

AD 61
Colossians ch.1 v15

AD 66
James ch.3 v9-10

Increase

Most popular Old Testament	Most popular New Testament
Psalms and Ezekiel.	Luke and 2 Corinthians.

If the book is missing, it would be **bold**	
	Gospels
Pentateuch	**Acts**
Joshua and Judges	Letters of Paul
History books	**Letter of James**
After captivity	**Letters of Peter**
Psalms	**Pastoral Epistles**
Proverbs and Ecclesiastes	**Hebrews**
Major prophets	**Revelation**
Minor prophets	

Missing books
Why is it not in Genesis?

Added books
Why is it in Ecclesiastes?

What meaning is there in the Old and New Testament
The word increase means gaining plenty more.

How many verses in the Old Testament	How many verses in the New Testament
Fifteen.	Two.

1240 BC
Leviticus ch.19 v25-26

1000 BC
Psalm ch.75 v10; ch.107 v38; ch.120 v3; ch.132 v17

975 BC
1 Chronicles ch.21 v3

950 BC
Eccleasiastes ch.1 v18

580 BC
Jeremiah ch.23 v3-4; ch.31 v27

570 BC
Ezekiel ch.36 v10-11, v37; ch.37 v26

530 BC
Daniel ch.11 v5; ch.12 v4

AD 30
Luke ch.17 v5

AD 55
2 Corinthians ch.9 v10

Interest

Most popular Old Testament Ezekiel.	Most popular New Testament Galatians.
If the book is missing, it would be **bold** Pentateuch **Joshua and Judges** History books After captivity Psalms Proverbs and Ecclesiastes Major prophets **Minor prophets**	Gospels **Acts** Letters of Paul **Letter of James** **Letters of Peter** **Pastoral Epistles** **Hebrews** **Revelation**
Missing books Why is it not in Isaiah and Jeremiah?	
Added books Why is it in Galatians?	
What meaning is there in the Old and New Testament They could not charge interest to another Israelite.	
How many verses in the Old Testament Twenty-one.	How many verses in the New Testament Five.

1680 BC
Genesis ch.12 v13

1280 BC
Exodus ch.22 v25-26

1240 BC
Leviticus ch.25 v36-38
Deuteronomy ch.23 v20

1000 BC
Psalm ch.15 v5

950 BC
Proverbs ch.18 v2

570 BC
Ezekiel ch.16 v5

465 BC
Esther ch.3 v8-9

400 BC
Nehemiah ch.5 v7

AD 30
Matthew ch.25 v27

AD 53
Philippians ch.2 v4

AD 54
Galatians ch.6 v14-15

Knee

Most popular Old Testament	Most popular New Testament
Isaiah.	Romans and Philippians.

If the book is missing, it would be **bold**	
Pentateuch	**Gospels**
Joshua and Judges	**Acts**
History books	Letters of Paul
After captivity	**Letter of James**
Psalms	**Letters of Peter**
Proverbs and Ecclesiastes	**Pastoral Epistles**
Major prophets	**Hebrews**
Minor prophets	**Revelation**

Missing books
Why is it not in Hebrews?

Added books
Why is it in the Letters of Paul?

What meaning is there in the Old and New Testament
Every knee will bow to Jesus.

How many verses in the Old Testament	How many verses in the New Testament
One.	Two.

685 BC
Isaiah ch.45 v23

AD 55
Romans ch.14 v11

AD 53
Philippians ch.2 v10

Knife

Most popular Old Testament	Most popular New Testament
Genesis.	None.

If the book is missing, it would be **bold**	
	Gospels
Pentateuch	**Acts**
Joshua and Judges	**Letters of Paul**
History books	**Letter of James**
After captivity	**Letters of Peter**
Psalms	**Pastoral Epistles**
Proverbs and Ecclesiastes	**Hebrews**
Major prophets	**Revelation**
Minor prophets	

Missing books
Why is it not in the New Testament?

Added books
Why is it in Genesis?

What meaning is there in the Old and New Testament
The word knife means a tool that can cut something.

How many verses in the Old Testament	How many verses in the New Testament
Six.	None.

1680 BC
Genesis ch.22 v6, v10

1280 BC
Exodus ch.4 v25

1060 BC
Judges ch.19 v29

950 BC
Proverbs ch.23 v2

580 BC
Jeremiah ch.36 v23

Knowledge

Most popular Old Testament	Most popular New Testament
Proverbs.	1 Corinthians.

If the book is missing, it would be **bold**	
Pentateuch	Gospels
Joshua and Judges	**Acts**
History books	Letters of Paul
After captivity	**Letter of James**
Psalms	Letters of Peter
Proverbs and Ecclesiastes	Pastoral Epistles
Major prophets	Hebrews
Minor prophets	**Revelation**

Missing books

Why is it not in Acts or Revelation?

Added books

Why is it in Proverbs?

What meaning is there in the Old and New Testament

God gives knowledge to the just.

How many verses in the Old Testament	How many verses in the New Testament
Fifty-eight.	Twenty-nine.

1680 BC
Genesis ch.2 v9

1300 BC
Job ch.11 v8; ch.36 v4

1240 BC
Numbers ch.24 v16

1000 BC
Psalm ch.119 v66

950 BC
Proverbs ch.1 v7; ch.2 v6
Ecclesiastes ch.2 v26

850 BC
1 Kings ch.4 v29-30

720 BC
Hosea ch.4 v1

685 BC
Isaiah ch.11 v2

580 BC
Jeremiah ch.3 v15

530 BC
Daniel ch.5 v12

445 BC
Malachi ch.2 v7

AD 30
Matthew ch.13 v12
Luke ch.11 v52

AD 53
1 Corinthians ch.12 v8; ch.14 v6
Philippians ch.1 v9

AD 55
Romans ch.11 v33

AD 61
Ephesians ch.4 v13
Colossians ch.1 v9

AD 64
2 Peter ch.1 v5

AD 66
Hebrews ch.10 v26

Lamp

Most popular Old Testament	Most popular New Testament
Exodus.	Luke.

If the book is missing, it would be **bold**	
Pentateuch	Gospels
Joshua and Judges	**Acts**
History books	**Letters of Paul**
After captivity	**Letter of James**
Psalms	Letters of Peter
Proverbs and Ecclesiastes	**Pastoral Epistles**
Major prophets	**Hebrews**
Minor prophets	Revelation

Missing books
Why is it not in the Letters of Paul?

Added books
Why is it in Exodus?

What meaning is there in the Old and New Testament
A lamp shines in the darkness.

How many verses in the Old Testament	How many verses in the New Testament
Twenty-eight.	Sixteen.

1300 BC
Job ch.18 v6

1280 BC
Exodus ch.25 v34, v38

1240 BC
Numbers ch.4 v9

1010 BC
1 Samuel ch.3 v3

1000 BC
Psalm ch.18 v28

975 BC
2 Samuel ch.22 v29

950 BC
Proverbs ch.6 v23; ch.31 v18

850 BC
1 Kings ch.11 v36; ch.15 v4

580 BC
2 Kings ch.4 v10; ch.8 v19
2 Chronicles ch.21 v7
Jeremiah ch.52 v18-19

AD 30
Matthew ch.5 v15-16; ch.6 v22-23
Luke ch.15 v8
John ch.5 v35

AD 80
2 Peter ch.1 v19

AD 96
Revelation ch.18 v23

Language

Most popular Old Testament Genesis and Daniel.	Most popular New Testament 1 Corinthians and Revelation.
If the book is missing, it would be **bold** Pentateuch **Joshua and Judges** History books After captivity **Psalms** **Proverbs and Ecclesiastes** Major prophets Minor prophets	**Gospels** Acts Letters of Paul **Letter of James** **Letters of Peter** **Pastoral Epistles** **Hebrews** Revelation
Missing books Why is it not in the Gospels?	
Added books Why is it in Daniel and Revelation?	
What meaning is there in the Old and New Testament In the beginning, all men spoke the same language.	
How many verses in the Old Testament Twenty-three.	How many verses in the New Testament Fourteen.

1680 BC
Genesis ch.10 v5; ch.11 v6

1240 BC
Deuteronomy ch.28 v49

685 BC
Isaiah ch.19 v18

580 BC
Jeremiah ch.5 v15

570 BC
Ezekiel ch.3 v5-8

530 BC
Daniel ch.1 v4

465 BC
Esther ch.1 v22

450 BC
Ezra ch.4 v7

400 BC
Nehemiah ch.13 v24

AD 53
1 Corinthians ch.14 v10-12

AD 61
Ephesians ch.4 v29
Colossians ch.3 v8-10

AD 63
Acts ch.22 v2

AD 96
Revelation ch.5 v9; ch.13 v7-8; ch.14 v6-7

Lawyer

Most popular Old Testament	Most popular New Testament
Jeremiah and Lamentations.	Acts and Titus.

If the book is missing, it would be **bold**	
	Gospels
Pentateuch	Acts
Joshua and Judges	Letters of Paul
History books	**Letter of James**
After captivity	**Letters of Peter**
Psalms	Pastoral Epistles
Proverbs and Ecclesiastes	**Hebrews**
Major prophets	**Revelation**
Minor prophets	

Missing books

Why is it not in Psalms and Proverbs?

Added books

Why is it in Jeremiah and Lamentations?

What meaning is there in the Old and New Testament

The lawyer presents the case against us.

How many verses in the Old Testament	How many verses in the New Testament
Two.	Two.

580 BC
Jeremiah ch.51 v36
Lamentations ch.3 v58-60

AD 63
Acts ch.24 v1-2

AD 64
Titus ch.3 v13-14

Lightning

Most popular Old Testament	Most popular New Testament
Job and Psalms.	Revelation.

If the book is missing, it would be **bold**	
Pentateuch	Gospels
Joshua and Judges	**Acts**
History books	**Letters of Paul**
After captivity	**Letter of James**
Psalms	**Letters of Peter**
Proverbs and Ecclesiastes	**Pastoral Epistles**
Major prophets	**Hebrews**
Minor prophets	Revelation

Missing books

Why is it not in the Letters of Paul, James and Peter?

Added books

Why is it in Job and Psalms?

What meaning is there in the Old and New Testament

God directs lightning and he controls it.

How many verses in the Old Testament	How many verses in the New Testament
Thirty-four.	Eight.

1300 BC
Job ch.36 v32-33; ch.37 v15-16; ch.38 v35

1280 BC
Exodus ch.9 v23; ch.19 v16; ch.20 v18

1000 BC
Psalm ch.29 v7; ch.97 v4

975 BC
2 Samuel ch.22 v15

580 BC
Jeremiah ch.10 v13

570 BC
Ezekiel ch.1 v4

515 BC
Zechariah ch.9 v14

AD 30
Matthew ch.24 v27
Luke ch.10 v18

AD 96
Revelation ch.8 v5; ch.11 v19

Linen

Most popular Old Testament	Most popular New Testament
Exodus.	Revelation.

If the book is missing, it would be **bold**	
	Gospels
Pentateuch	**Acts**
Joshua and Judges	**Letters of Paul**
History books	**Letter of James**
After captivity	**Letters of Peter**
Psalms	**Pastoral Epistles**
Proverbs and Ecclesiastes	**Hebrews**
Major prophets	Revelation
Minor prophets	

Missing books
Why is it not in the Psalms?

Added books
Why is it in Revelation?

What meaning is there in the Old and New Testament
Fine linen represents the good deeds of God's people.

How many verses in the Old Testament	How many verses in the New Testament
Eighty-three.	Fourteen.

1680 BC
Genesis ch.41 v42-43

1280 BC
Exodus ch.26 v1-2; ch.39 v27-29

1240 BC
Leviticus ch.13 v47-49; ch.16 v23-24
Deuteronomy ch.22 v11

1060 BC
Judges ch.14 v12-13

975 BC
1 Chronicles ch.4 v21-22; ch.15 v27

950 BC
Proverbs ch.7 v16; ch.31 v24

720 BC
Hosea ch.2 v5

685 BC
Isaiah ch.3 v18-23

580 BC
2 Chronicles ch.5 v12-13
Jeremiah ch.13 v1-2

570 BC
Ezekiel ch.9 v3-4

530 BC
Daniel ch.12 v6

465 BC
Esther ch.1 v6; ch.8 v15

AD 30
Matthew ch.27 v59-60
Mark ch.14 v51-52
Luke ch.16 v19
John ch.19 v40-41

AD 96
Revelation ch.15 v6-7; ch.19 v8

Lion

Most popular Old Testament	Most popular New Testament
1 Kings.	Revelation.

If the book is missing, it would be **bold**	
	Gospels
Pentateuch	**Acts**
Joshua and Judges	**Letters of Paul**
History books	**Letter of James**
After captivity	Letters of Peter
Psalms	**Pastoral Epistles**
Proverbs and Ecclesiastes	**Hebrews**
Major prophets	Revelation
Minor prophets	

Missing books

Why is it not in the Letters of Paul?

Added books

Why is it in Jeremiah?

What meaning is there in the Old and New Testament

The lion is a ferocious beast; nothing can make him afraid.

How many verses in the Old Testament	How many verses in the New Testament
Sixty-six.	Six.

1680 BC
Genesis ch.49 v9

1300 BC
Job ch.4 v10-11; ch.10 v16

1240 BC
Numbers ch.23 v24; ch.24 v9

1060 BC
Judges ch.14 v5-6

1010 BC
1 Samuel ch.17 v34-36

1000 BC
Psalm ch.7 v2

975 BC
2 Samuel ch.17 v10; ch.23 v20

950 BC
Proverbs ch.26 v13; ch.30 v30
Ecclesiastes ch.9 v4

850 BC
1 Kings ch.10 v19; ch.13 v26; ch.20 v36

750 BC
Amos ch.3 v8; ch.5 v19

720 BC
Hosea ch.5 v14; ch.11 v10-11

690 BC
Micah ch.5 v8

685 BC
Isaiah ch.11 v7; ch.31 v4

630 BC
Nahum ch.2 v12

580 BC
Jeremiah ch.2 v30; ch.12 v8
Lamentations ch.3 v10

570 BC
Ezekiel ch.19 v3; ch.32 v2

AD 64
1 Peter ch.5 v8-9

AD 96
Revelation ch.5 v5; ch.10 v3; ch.13 v2

Loaf

Most popular Old Testament	Most popular New Testament
Exodus, Leviticus, Judges, 2 Samuel, 1 Chronicles and Jeremiah.	Matthew, Mark, Luke, 1 Corinthians and Revelation.
If the book is missing, it would be **bold** Pentateuch Joshua and Judges History books **After captivity** **Psalms** **Proverbs and Ecclesiastes** Major prophets **Minor prophets**	Gospels **Acts** Letters of Paul **Letter of James** **Letters of Peter** **Pastoral Epistles** **Hebrews** Revelation

Missing books Why is it not in Isaiah?
Added books Why it is in Revelation?
What meaning is there in the Old and New Testament A loaf is something to eat.

| How many verses in the Old Testament

Six. | How many verses in the New Testament

Five. |

1280 BC
Exodus ch.29 v23

1240 BC
Leviticus ch.2 v5-7

1060 BC
Judges ch.7 v13

1010 BC
2 Samuel ch.6 v19

975 BC
1 Chronicles ch.16 v34

580 BC
Jeremiah ch.37 v21

AD 30
Matthew ch.7 v9
Mark ch.8 v14
Luke ch.4 v3

AD 53
1 Corinthians ch.10 v17

AD 96
Revelation ch.6 v6

Loan

Most popular Old Testament	Most popular New Testament
Deuteronomy.	None.

If the book is missing, it would be **bold**	
	Gospels
Pentateuch	**Acts**
Joshua and Judges	**Letters of Paul**
History books	**Letter of James**
After captivity	**Letters of Peter**
Psalms	**Pastoral Epistles**
Proverbs and Ecclesiastes	**Hebrews**
Major prophets	**Revelation**
Minor prophets	

Missing books Why is it not in the New Testament?

Added books Why is it in Deuteronomy?

What meaning is there in the Old and New Testament If you are poor, you will have to take a loan to get money.

How many verses in the Old Testament	How many verses in the New Testament
Nine.	None.

1300 BC
Job ch.24 v3-4, v9-11

1280 BC
Exodus ch.22 v26-27

1240 BC
Deuteronomy ch.15 v9-10; ch.23 v19-20; ch.24 v6, v12-3

570 BC
Ezekiel ch.22 v12-13

Lot

Most popular Old Testament	Most popular New Testament
1 Chronicles.	Luke.

If the book is missing, it would be **bold**	
Pentateuch	Gospels
Joshua and Judges	Acts
History books	Letters of Paul
After captivity	**Letter of James**
Psalms	Letters of Peter
Proverbs and Ecclesiastes	**Pastoral Epistles**
Major prophets	**Hebrews**
Minor prophets	**Revelation**

Missing books

Why is it not in Matthew and Mark's Gospels?

Added books

Why is it in Genesis?

What meaning is there in the Old and New Testament

The word lot can refer to a man or other things.

How many verses in the Old Testament	How many verses in the New Testament
One hundred and Nine.	Eleven.

1680 BC
Genesis ch.12 v5; ch.13 v14; ch.14 v12; ch.19 v16

1300 BC
Job ch.11 v2; ch.30 v2

1280 BC
Exodus ch.16 v17

1240 BC
Leviticus ch.16 v10
Numbers ch.26 v56; ch.34 v13

1010 BC
1 Samuel ch.25 v21

975 BC
2 Samuel ch.18 v29

950 BC
Proverbs ch.1 v14
Ecclesiastes ch.5 v19; ch.7 v4

685 BC
Isaiah ch.24 v17

580 BC
Jeremiah ch.48 v43

570 BC
Ezekiel ch.3 v7

AD 30
Luke ch.1 v9
John ch.2 v10; ch.7 v12

AD 53
1 Corinthians ch.4 v20

AD 63
Acts ch.16 v16; ch.27 v9

AD 80
2 Peters ch.2 v8

Lust

Most popular Old Testament	Most popular New Testament
Job.	Matthew.

If the book is missing, it would be **bold**	
Pentateuch **Joshua and Judges** **History books** **After captivity** **Psalms** Proverbs and Ecclesiastes Major prophets Minor prophets	Gospels **Acts** Letters of Paul **Letter of James** Letters of Peter **Pastoral Epistles** **Hebrews** **Revelation**

Missing books
Why is it not in the Psalms?

Added books
Why is it in the Matthew's Gospel?

What meaning is there in the Old and New Testament
Lust means giving up for God the evil habits.

How many verses in the Old Testament	How many verses in the New Testament
Ten.	Seven.

1280 BC
Exodus ch.34 v15

1300 BC
Job ch.22 v24; ch.31 v1, v11

950 BC
Proverbs ch.6 v25

720 BC
Hosea ch.7 v4

580 BC
Jeremiah ch.2 v24; ch.13 v27

570 BC
Ezekiel ch.16 v36-37; ch.23 v11-12

AD 30
Matthew ch.5 v28-29

AD 53
1 Corinthians ch.7 v9

AD 55
Romans ch.1 v27

AD 61
Ephesians ch.4 v22-24
Colossians ch.3 v5

AD 64
1 Peter ch.4 v3

Magic

Most popular Old Testament	Most popular New Testament
Ezekiel.	Acts.

If the book is missing, it would be **bold**	
Pentateuch	**Gospels**
Joshua and Judges	Acts
History books	**Letters of Paul**
After captivity	**Letter of James**
Psalms	**Letters of Peter**
Proverbs and Ecclesiastes	**Pastoral Epistles**
Major prophets	**Hebrews**
Minor prophets	**Revelation**

Missing books

Why is it not in Genesis or Revelation?

Added books

Why is it in Acts?

What meaning is there in the Old and New Testament

The Lord God says magic is wrong.

How many verses in the Old Testament	How many verses in the New Testament
Eleven.	One.

1280 BC
Exodus ch.7 v11, v22; ch.8 v7

1240 BC
Numbers ch.23 v23

1220 BC
Joshua ch.13 v22

685 BC
Isaiah ch.47 v9

570 BC
Ezekiel ch.13 v18, v20-21

630 BC
Nahum ch.3 v4

AD 63
Acts ch.8 v11

Manna

Most popular Old Testament	Most popular New Testament
Exodus.	John.

If the book is missing, it would be **bold**	
Pentateuch	Gospels
Joshua and Judges	**Acts**
History books	**Letters of Paul**
After captivity	**Letter of James**
Psalms	**Letters of Peter**
Proverbs and Ecclesiastes	**Pastoral Epistles**
Major prophets	Hebrews
Minor prophets	Revelation

Missing books

Why is it not in the Major and Minor Prophets?

Added books

Why is it in John's Gospel?

What meaning is there in the Old and New Testament

Manna is what God produced to let the Israelites feed.

How many verses in the Old Testament	How many verses in the New Testament
Seventeen.	Five.

1280 BC
Exodus ch.16 v31, v35

1240 BC
Numbers ch.11 v7-9; ch.21 v5
Deuteronomy ch.8 v3-4, v16-17

1220 BC
Joshua ch.5 v12

1000 BC
Psalm ch.78 v24; ch.105 v40

400 BC
Nehemiah ch.9 v20

AD 30
John ch.6 v31, v49-50

AD 66
Hebrews ch.9 v4-5

AD 96
Revelation ch.2 v17

Mark

Most popular Old Testament	Most popular New Testament
Genesis.	Acts and Revelation.

If the book is missing, it would be **bold**	
	Gospels
Pentateuch	Acts
Joshua and Judges	Letters of Paul
History books	**Letter of James**
After captivity	Letters of Peter
Psalms	Pastoral Epistles
Proverbs and Ecclesiastes	Hebrews
Major prophets	Revelation
Minor prophets	

Missing books
Why is it not in Isaiah?

Added books
Why is it in Revelation?

What meaning is there in the Old and New Testament
There were numerous references to mark.

How many verses in the Old Testament	How many verses in the New Testament
Twenty-two.	Twenty-three.

1680 BC
Genesis ch.1 v14-16; ch.4 v15; ch.17 v13-14; ch.35 v14

1300 BC
Job ch.14 v13

1280 BC
Exodus ch.13 v9; ch.19 v12

1240 BC
Leviticus ch.19 v28
Deuteronomy ch.19 v14

1000 BC
Psalm ch.104 v19

950 BC
Proverbs ch.4 v26; ch.20 v3

850 BC
1 Kings ch.22 v28

580 BC
Jeremiah ch.50 v9

570 BC
Ezekiel ch.9 v4

AD 30
Matthew ch.26 v29

AD 61
Colossians ch.4 v10

AD 63
Acts ch.12 v25

AD 64
2 Timothy ch.4 v11

AD 66
Hebrews ch.12 v13

AD 96
Revelation ch.13 v16-17; ch.14 v9-10

Market

Most popular Old Testament	Most popular New Testament
Genesis and Zephaniah.	Mark.

If the book is missing, it would be **bold**	
Pentateuch	Gospels
Joshua and Judges	**Acts**
History books	**Letters of Paul**
After captivity	**Letter of James**
Psalms	**Letters of Peter**
Proverbs and Ecclesiastes	**Pastoral Epistles**
Major prophets	**Hebrews**
Minor prophets	**Revelation**

Missing books

Why is it not in the Letters of Paul, James and Peter?

Added books

Why is it in Zephaniah?

What meaning is there in the Old and New Testament

The transactions were done in the market.

How many verses in the Old Testament	How many verses in the New Testament
Two.	One.

1680 BC
Genesis ch.23 v16

625 BC
Zephaniah ch.1 v11

AD 30
Mark ch.7 v4

Meal

Most popular Old Testament	Most popular New Testament
Genesis.	Luke.

If the book is missing, it would be **bold**	
	Gospels
Pentateuch	Acts
Joshua and Judges	Letters of Paul
History books	**Letter of James**
After captivity	Letters of Peter
Psalms	**Pastoral Epistles**
Proverbs and Ecclesiastes	Hebrews
Major prophets	Revelation
Minor prophets	

Missing books
Why is it not in Psalms or John?

Added books
Why is it in Luke's Gospel?

What meaning is there in the Old and New Testament
The act of taking food is a meal.

How many verses in the Old Testament	How many verses in the New Testament
Twenty-eight.	Twenty-four.

1680 BC
Genesis ch.24 v54; ch.25 v34; ch.27 v7-10; ch.31 v46

1280 BC
Exodus ch.12 v11; ch.18 v12

1150 BC
Ruth ch.2 v18

1010 BC
1 Samuel ch.1 v9; ch.20 v27

950 BC
Proverbs ch.13 v2; ch.18 v20

850 BC
1 Kings ch.17 v12

580 BC
2 Chronicles ch.30 v18
Jeremiah ch.16 v7

400 BC
Nehemiah ch.8 v12

AD 30
Matthew ch.8 v15; ch.26 v18-19
Luke ch.22 v16

AD 53
1 Corinthians ch.11 v21

AD 63
Acts ch.10 v9-10; ch.16 v34

AD 64
1 Peter ch.4 v9

AD 96
Revelation ch.3 v20

Measure

Most popular Old Testament	Most popular New Testament
Ezekiel.	Revelation.

If the book is missing, it would be **bold**	
Pentateuch	**Gospels**
Joshua and Judges	**Acts**
History books	**Letters of Paul**
After captivity	**Letter of James**
Psalms	**Letters of Peter**
Proverbs and Ecclesiastes	**Pastoral Epistles**
Major prophets	**Hebrews**
Minor prophets	Revelation

Missing books

Why is it not in Jeremiah?

Added books

Why is it in Revelation?

What meaning is there in the Old and New Testament

There were numerous references to measure.

How many verses in the Old Testament	How many verses in the New Testament
Twenty-four.	Three.

1680 BC
Genesis ch.41 v49

1280 BC
Exodus ch.16 v36

1240 BC
Numbers ch.35 v5
Deuteronomy ch.21 v2

1000 BC
Psalm ch.28 v4; ch.145 v3

850 BC
1 Kings ch.7 v9-10

750 BC
Amos ch.8 v5-6

720 BC
Hosea ch.3 v2

580 BC
2 Kings ch.21 v13-14
2 Chronicles ch.11 v12

685 BC
Isaiah ch.34 v11

570 BC
Ezekiel ch.4 v11; ch.48 v16

515 BC
Zechariah ch.2 v2

AD 63
Revelation ch.11 v1-2; ch.21 v15

Mediator

Most popular Old Testament	Most popular New Testament
Job.	Galatians.
If the book is missing, it would be **bold**	**Gospels**
Pentateuch	**Acts**
Joshua and Judges	Letters of Paul
History books	**Letter of James**
After captivity	**Letters of Peter**
Psalms	Pastoral Epistles
Proverbs and Ecclesiastes	**Hebrews**
Major prophets	**Revelation**
Minor prophets	

Missing books
Why is it not in the Major Prophets?

Added books
Why is it in the Letters of Paul?

What meaning is there in the Old and New Testament
Jesus is a mediator for us to talk to God.

How many verses in the Old Testament	How many verses in the New Testament
Two.	Four.

1300 BC
Job ch.9 v33-35

AD 54
Galatians ch.3 v19-20

AD 64
1 Timothy ch.2 v5-6

Medicine

Most popular Old Testament Jeremiah.	Most popular New Testament Revelation.
If the book is missing, it would be **bold** **Pentateuch** **Joshua and Judges** History books **After captivity** Psalms Proverbs and Ecclesiastes Major prophets **Minor prophets**	**Gospels** **Acts** **Letters of Paul** **Letter of James** **Letters of Peter** **Pastoral Epistles** **Hebrews** Revelation
Missing books Why is it not in the Pentateuch?	
Added books Why is it in Jeremiah?	
What meaning is there in the Old and New Testament Medicine is there for people to heal themselves.	
How many verses in the Old Testament Seven.	How many verses in the New Testament One.

1000 BC
Psalm ch.141 v5

975 BC
2 Samuel ch.16 v8

950 BC
Proverbs ch.17 v22

580 BC
Jeremiah ch.8 v22; ch.30 v13; ch.46 v11; ch.51 v8-9

AD 96
Revelation ch.22 v2

Mercy

Most popular Old Testament	Most popular New Testament
Psalms.	Matthew.

If the book is missing, it would be **bold**	
Pentateuch	Gospels
Joshua and Judges	**Acts**
History books	Letters of Paul
After captivity	Letter of James
Psalms	Letters of Peter
Proverbs and Ecclesiastes	Pastoral Epistles
Major prophets	Hebrews
Minor prophets	**Revelation**

Missing books

Why is it not in Acts or Revelation?

Added books

Why is it in Isaiah?

What meaning is there in the Old and New Testament

Mercy is from God alone.

How many verses in the Old Testament	How many verses in the New Testament
One hundred and Fourteen.	Fifty-eight.

1300 BC
Job ch.9 v15-16

1280 BC
Exodus ch.1 v13-14; ch.33 v19-20; ch.34 v6

1240 BC
Deuteronomy ch.7 v2-3; ch.30 v3-4

1220 BC
Joshua ch.11 v20

1010 BC
1 Samuel ch.9 v16

1000 BC
Psalm ch.25 v16; ch.31 v22

975 BC
2 Samuel ch.24 v14

950 BC
Proverbs ch.6 v34-35; ch.28 v13

690 BC
Micah ch.6 v8

685 BC
Isaiah ch.13 v18; ch.49 v10

580 BC
2 Chronicles ch.28 v9-11
Jeremiah ch.11 v11-12
Lamentations ch.3 v43

570 BC
Ezekiel ch.9 v5-6

530 BC
Daniel ch.9 v13-14

515 BC
Zechariah ch.7 v9-10

450 BC
Ezra ch.9 v7

400 BC
Nehemiah ch.9 v19-21

AD 30
Matthew ch.5 v7; ch.12 v7; ch.23 v23

AD 54
Galatians ch.6 v16

AD 55
Romans ch.1 v31-32; ch.9 v15-16, v18; ch.11 v31-32

AD 61
Ephesians ch.2 v4-5
Colossians ch.3 v12

AD 64
2 Timothy ch.1 v2

AD 66
Hebrews ch.10 v29
James ch.2 v13; ch.5 v11

AD 80
Jude ch.1 v2

Messiah

Most popular Old Testament	Most popular New Testament
Isaiah.	Matthew.

If the book is missing, it would be **bold**	
Pentateuch	Gospels
Joshua and Judges	Acts
History books	**Letters of Paul**
After captivity	**Letter of James**
Psalms	**Letters of Peter**
Proverbs and Ecclesiastes	**Pastoral Epistles**
Major prophets	**Hebrews**
Minor prophets	**Revelation**

Missing books

Why is it not in the Letters of Paul?

Added books

Why is it in Isaiah?

What meaning is there in the Old and New Testament

Jesus is the Messiah.

How many verses in the Old Testament	How many verses in the New Testament
One.	Ninety-eight.

AD 30

Matthew ch.1 v1, v18-19; ch.12 v23; ch.16 v16; ch.22 v41-45; ch.23 v10, v63-64

John ch.7 v31

AD 63

Acts ch.2 v36; ch.3 v18; ch.17 v3; ch.18 v28

Metal

Most popular Old Testament	Most popular New Testament
Numbers.	None.

If the book is missing, it would be **bold**	
Pentateuch	**Gospels**
Joshua and Judges	**Acts**
History books	**Letters of Paul**
After captivity	**Letter of James**
Psalms	**Letters of Peter**
Proverbs and Ecclesiastes	**Pastoral Epistles**
Major prophets	**Hebrews**
Minor prophets	**Revelation**

Missing books

Why is it not in the New Testament?

Added books

Why is it in Numbers?

What meaning is there in the Old and New Testament

A metal can be gold, silver, bronze, iron, tin or lead.

How many verses in the Old Testament	How many verses in the New Testament
Ten.	None.

1280 BC
Exodus ch.34 v17

1240 BC
Leviticus ch.19 v4
Numbers ch.16 v38; ch.31 v21-23

850 BC
1 Kings ch.7 v14

685 BC
Isaiah ch.48 v5-6

580 BC
2 Kings ch.17 v16
2 Chronicles ch.28 v2-3
Jeremiah ch.9 v7

445 BC
Malachi ch.3 v2-4

Mildew

Most popular Old Testament	Most popular New Testament
Leviticus.	None.

If the book is missing, it would be **bold**	
	Gospels
Pentateuch	**Acts**
Joshua and Judges	**Letters of Paul**
History books	**Letter of James**
After captivity	**Letters of Peter**
Psalms	**Pastoral Epistles**
Proverbs and Ecclesiastes	**Hebrews**
Major prophets	**Revelation**
Minor prophets	

Missing books
Why is it not in the New Testament?

Added books
Why is it in Leviticus?

What meaning is there in the Old and New Testament
The Lord sends mildew and blight.

How many verses in the Old Testament	How many verses in the New Testament
Twenty.	None.

1240 BC
Leviticus ch.13 v52, v56-57; ch.14 v34-37, v39-42, v44-47, v54-57
Deuteronomy ch.28 v22-24

750 BC
Amos ch.4 v9

515 BC
Haggai ch.2 v17

Minister

Most popular Old Testament	Most popular New Testament
Ezekiel.	None.
If the book is missing, it would be **bold**	
Pentateuch **Joshua and Judges** History books After captivity **Psalms** **Proverbs and Ecclesiastes** Major prophets Minor prophets	**Gospels** **Acts** **Letters of Paul** **Letter of James** **Letters of Peter** **Pastoral Epistles** **Hebrews** **Revelation**
Missing books Why is it not in the New Testament?	
Added books Why is it in Ezekiel?	
What meaning is there in the Old and New Testament The priests and Levites minister before God.	
How many verses in the Old Testament Twenty-one.	How many verses in the New Testament None

1280 BC
Exodus ch.28 v1-2; ch.39 v41

1240 BC
Numbers ch.3 v3; ch.16 v8-10
Deuteronomy ch.18 v5; ch.21 v5

975 BC
1 Chronicles ch.16 v39

580 BC
2 Chronicles ch.29 v11
Jeremiah ch.33 v21-22

570 BC
Ezekiel ch.43 v19-20; ch.44 v15-16; ch.45 v4-5

550 BC
Joel ch.2 v17

465 BC
Esther ch.10 v3

400 BC
Nehemiah ch.10 v36

Ministry

Most popular Old Testament	Most popular New Testament
Numbers and Deuteronomy.	2 Corinthians.

If the book is missing, it would be **bold**	
Pentateuch	Gospels
Joshua and Judges	Acts
History books	Letters of Paul
After captivity	**Letter of James**
Psalms	**Letters of Peter**
Proverbs and Ecclesiastes	Pastoral Epistles
Major prophets	Hebrews
Minor prophets	**Revelation**

Missing books
Why is it not in Revelation?

Added books
Why is it in 2 Corinthians?

What meaning is there in the Old and New Testament
A minister is a person who administers something.

How many verses in the Old Testament	How many verses in the New Testament
Two.	Twenty-five.

1240 BC
Numbers ch.16 v10
Deuteronomy ch.33 v11

AD 30
Mark ch.4 v34; ch.6 v30
Luke ch.3 v23
John ch.11 v54; ch.13 v1; ch.15 v27

AD 63
Acts ch.1 v24-25; ch.21 v19

AD 55
Romans ch.16 v3
2 Corinthians ch.5 v12; ch.6 v3; ch.8 v6

AD 64
2 Timothy ch.4 v5

AD 66
Hebrews ch.8 v6

Money

Most popular Old Testament	Most popular New Testament
Genesis.	Luke.

If the book is missing, it would be **bold**	
Pentateuch	Gospels
Joshua and Judges	Acts
History books	Letters of Paul
After captivity	**Letter of James**
Psalms	Letters of Peter
Proverbs and Ecclesiastes	Pastoral Epistles
Major prophets	Hebrews
Minor prophets	**Revelation**

Missing books
Why is it not in Revelation?

Added books
Why is it in 2 Kings?

What meaning is there in the Old and New Testament
Money is the same as legal tender.

How many verses in the Old Testament	How many verses in the New Testament
One hundred and Fourteen.	Seventy.

1680 BC
Genesis ch.42 v35

1300 BC
Job ch.22 v24; ch.31 v24-25

1280 BC
Exodus ch.30 v16

1240 BC
Leviticus ch.6 v4-6
Deuteronomy ch.15 v1

1010 BC
1 Samuel ch.8 v3

1000 BC
Psalm ch.112 v5; ch.119 v36

975 BC
2 Samuel ch.8 v6

950 BC
Proverbs ch.1 v19; ch.10 v16
Ecclesiastes ch.5 v10-11; ch.7 v12

690 BC
Micah ch.6 v14

685 BC
Isaiah ch.55 v2

620 BC
Habakkuk ch.2 v9

580 BC
2 Kings ch.5 v26-27; ch.12 v7-8, v15-16
2 Chronicles ch.24 v10

570 BC
Ezekiel ch.18 v13

515 BC
Zechariah ch.8 v10

400 BC
Nehemiah ch.5 v4-5

AD 30
Matthew ch.6 v24; ch.19 v21-22; ch.26 v8-9
Mark ch.12 v41-42
Luke ch.3 v14; ch.14 v28-29; ch.15 v13-15; ch.22 v5-6
John ch.12 v6

AD 53
1 Corinthians ch.16 v2

AD 63
Acts ch.2 v45; ch.24 v17

AD 64
1 Timothy ch.3 v3; ch.6 v10, v17-19

AD 66
Hebrews ch.13 v5

AD 80
2 Peter ch.2 v3

AD 93
1 John ch.3 v17

Moon

Most popular Old Testament	Most popular New Testament
Psalms.	Revelation.

If the book is missing, it would be **bold**	
	Gospels
Pentateuch	Acts
Joshua and Judges	Letters of Paul
History books	**Letter of James**
After captivity	**Letters of Peter**
Psalms	**Pastoral Epistles**
Proverbs and Ecclesiastes	**Hebrews**
Major prophets	Revelation
Minor prophets	

Missing books

Why is it not in Hebrews?

Added books

Why is it in Revelation?

What meaning is there in the Old and New Testament

God creates the moon, and sets the seasons.

How many verses in the Old Testament	How many verses in the New Testament
Fifty-two.	Ten.

1680 BC
Genesis ch.1 v16-17

1300 BC
Job ch.25 v5; ch.26 v9

1240 BC
Deuteronomy ch.4 v19-20

1220 BC
Joshua ch.10 v13

1010 BC
1 Samuel ch.20 v5-6

1000 BC
Psalm ch.8 v3-4; ch.72 v7; ch.104 v19

950 BC
Ecclesiastes ch.12 v2-3

720 BC
Hosea ch.2 v11

685 BC
Isaiah ch.1 v14-15; ch.30 v26; ch.60 v20

625 BC
Zephaniah ch.1 v5-6

580 BC
2 Chronicles ch.8 v13
Jeremiah ch.31 v35

570 BC
Ezekiel ch.32 v7-8

550 BC
Joel ch.2 v31

450 BC
Ezra ch.3 v5

AD 30
Matthew ch.24 v29

AD 53
1 Corinthians ch.15 v41

AD 61
Colossians ch.2 v16-18

AD 96
Revelation ch.6 v12-14; ch.21 v23-24

Mouth

Most popular Old Testament	Most popular New Testament
Proverbs.	Revelation.

If the book is missing, it would be **bold**	
Pentateuch	Gospels
Joshua and Judges	Acts
History books	Letters of Paul
After captivity	Letter of James
Psalms	**Letters of Peter**
Proverbs and Ecclesiastes	**Pastoral Epistles**
Major prophets	**Hebrews**
Minor prophets	Revelation

Missing books
Why is it not in John's Gospel?

Added books
Why is it in Job?

What meaning is there in the Old and New Testament
God speaks what is true, and you can't control your mouth.

How many verses in the Old Testament	How many verses in the New Testament
Eighty-nine.	Twenty-five.

1300 BC
Job ch.9 v20; ch.37 v3-4

1280 BC
Exodus ch.4 v1-12

1240 BC
Leviticus ch.13 v45-46
Numbers ch.16 v32-33
Deuteronomy ch.8 v3; ch.18 v18

1060 BC
Judges ch.9 v38

1010 BC
1 Samuel ch.17 v34-36

1000 BC
Psalm ch.19 v14

975 BC
2 Samuel ch.16 v23

950 BC
Proverbs ch.2 v6; ch.10 v31-32
Ecclesiastes ch.5 v1, v6

750 BC
Amos ch.3 v12

685 BC
Isaiah ch.51 v16

580 BC
2 Kings ch.4 v34-35; ch.19 v28
Jeremiah ch.1 v8-9

570 BC
Ezekiel ch.3 v2-3

530 BC
Daniel ch.4 v31-32

AD 30
Matthew ch.15 v11
Mark ch.9 v20

AD 50
2 Thessalonians ch.2 v8

AD 55
Romans ch.10 v9-11

AD 63
Acts ch.8 v32-33

AD 66
James ch.3 v10-11

AD 96
Revelation ch.19 v15-16

Music

Most popular Old Testament Psalms.	Most popular New Testament Matthew, Luke and Ephesians.
If the book is missing, it would be **bold** Pentateuch Joshua and Judges History books After captivity Psalms **Proverbs and Ecclesiastes** Major prophets Minor prophets	Gospels **Acts** Letters of Paul **Letter of James** **Letters of Peter** **Pastoral Epistles** **Hebrews** **Revelation**

Missing books Why is it not in Jeremiah?	

Added books Why is it in Ephesians?	

What meaning is there in the Old and New Testament Music is important to the Jews and Christians.	

How many verses in the Old Testament Twenty-one.	How many verses in the New Testament Three.

1680 BC
Genesis ch.31 v27

1300 BC
Job ch.30 v31

1060 BC
Judges ch.5 v3

1010 BC
1 Samuel ch.16 v16

1000 BC
Psalm ch.27 v6; ch.135 v3

975 BC
1 Chronicles ch.6 v31-33; ch.25 v6-8

750 BC
Amos ch.5 v23-24

685 BC
Isaiah ch.5 v12

580 BC
2 Chronicles ch.7 v6; ch.20 v28

570 BC
Ezekiel ch.26 v13; ch.33 v32-33

400 BC
Nehemiah ch.12 v27-29

AD 30
Matthew ch.9 v23-25
Luke ch.15 v25-27

AD 61
Ephesians ch.5 v19-20

Mystery

Most popular Old Testament	Most popular New Testament
Ecclesiastes and Daniel.	1 Timothy and Revelation.

If the book is missing, it would be **bold**	
	Gospels
Pentateuch	**Acts**
Joshua and Judges	Letters of Paul
History books	**Letter of James**
After captivity	**Letters of Peter**
Psalms	Pastoral Epistles
Proverbs and Ecclesiastes	**Hebrews**
Major prophets	Revelation
Minor prophets	

Missing books

Why is it not in the Gospels?

Added books

Why is it in Ecclesiastes?

What meaning is there in the Old and New Testament

A mystery is a hidden concept.

How many verses in the Old Testament	How many verses in the New Testament
Two.	Seven.

950 BC
Ecclesiastes ch.11 v5

530 BC
Daniel ch.4 v9

AD 53
1 Corinthians ch.2 v7

AD 55
Romans ch.11 v25

AD 61
Ephesians ch.5 v32-33

AD 64
1 Timothy ch.3 v9-10, v16

AD 96
Revelation ch.1 v20; ch.17 v7-8

Nest

Most popular Old Testament	Most popular New Testament
Isaiah.	None.

If the book is missing, it would be **bold**	
	Gospels
Pentateuch	**Acts**
Joshua and Judges	**Letters of Paul**
History books	**Letter of James**
After captivity	**Letters of Peter**
Psalms	**Pastoral Epistles**
Proverbs and Ecclesiastes	**Hebrews**
Major prophets	**Revelation**
Minor prophets	

Missing books
Why is it not in the New Testament?

Added books
Why is it in Habbakuk?

What meaning is there in the Old and New Testament
A nest holds the bird's young.

How many verses in the Old Testament	How many verses in the New Testament
Fifteen.	None.

1300 BC
Job ch.39 v27

1240 BC
Numbers ch.24 v21-22
Deuteronomy ch.22 v6-7

1000 BC
Psalm ch.84 v3; ch.104 v12

950 BC
Proverbs ch.27 v8

685 BC
Isaiah ch.11 v8; ch.31 v5; ch.34 v15

580 BC
Jeremiah ch.48 v28; ch.49 v16

570 BC
Ezekiel ch.17 v23-24
Obadiah ch.1 v4

515 BC
Habbakuk ch.2 v9

Nettles

Most popular Old Testament	Most popular New Testament
Isaiah.	None.
If the book is missing, it would be **bold**	**Gospels**
Pentateuch	**Acts**
Joshua and Judges	**Letters of Paul**
History books	**Letter of James**
After captivity	**Letters of Peter**
Psalms	**Pastoral Epistles**
Proverbs and Ecclesiastes	**Hebrews**
Major prophets	**Revelation**
Minor prophets	

Missing books
Why is it not in Jeremiah?

Added books
Why is it in Isaiah?

What meaning is there in the Old and New Testament
Nettles, weeds and thistles where the Israelites lived and worked.

How many verses in the Old Testament	How many verses in the New Testament
Seven.	None.

1300 BC
Job ch.30 v7-8

950 BC
Proverbs ch.24 v31

720 BC
Hosea ch.9 v6

685 BC
Isaiah ch.34 v13; ch.55 v13

625 BC
Zephaniah ch.2 v9

570 BC
Ezekiel ch.2 v6-7

Nile

Most popular Old Testament	Most popular New Testament
Exodus.	None.

If the book is missing, it would be **bold**	
Pentateuch	**Gospels**
Joshua and Judges	**Acts**
History books	**Letters of Paul**
After captivity	**Letter of James**
Psalms	**Letters of Peter**
Proverbs and Ecclesiastes	**Pastoral Epistles**
Major prophets	**Hebrews**
Minor prophets	**Revelation**

Missing books
Why is it not in Revelation?

Added books
Why is it in Isaiah?

What meaning is there in the Old and New Testament
The river Nile flows through Egypt.

How many verses in the Old Testament	How many verses in the New Testament
Thirty-four.	None.

1680 BC
Genesis ch.41 v17

1280 BC
Exodus ch.1 v22; ch.2 v3; ch.7 v15-16; ch.8 v11; ch.17 v5-6

750 BC
Amos ch.9 v5

685 BC
Isaiah ch.18 v1; ch.19 v5-6; ch.23 v3

630 BC
Nahum ch.3 v8

580 BC
Jeremiah ch.2 v18-19

570 BC
Ezekiel ch.29 v3; ch.30 v12

515 BC
Zechariah ch.10 v11

Nomads

Most popular Old Testament Ezekiel.	Most popular New Testament Hebrews.
If the book is missing, it would be **bold** **Pentateuch** **Joshua and Judges** **History books** **After captivity** Psalms **Proverbs and Ecclesiastes** Major prophets **Minor prophets**	**Gospels** **Acts** **Letters of Paul** **Letter of James** **Letters of Peter** **Pastoral Epistles** Hebrews **Revelation**
Missing books Why is it not in the Proverbs?	
Added books Why is it in Hebrews?	
What meaning is there in the Old and New Testament Nomads are a wandering pastoral community.	
How many verses in the Old Testament Four.	How many verses in the New Testament One.

1000 BC
Psalm ch.72 v9

685 BC
Isaiah ch.13 v20

570 BC
Ezekiel ch.25 v3-4, v10

AD 66
Hebrews ch.11 v13-14

Oaths

Most popular Old Testament	Most popular New Testament
Deuteronomy, Isaiah, Hosea and Amos.	None.
If the book is missing, it would be **bold** Pentateuch **Joshua and Judges** **History books** **After captivity** **Psalms** **Proverbs and Ecclesiastes** Major prophets Minor prophets	**Gospels** **Acts** **Letters of Paul** **Letter of James** **Letters of Peter** **Pastoral Epistles** **Hebrews** **Revelation**

Missing books
Why is it not in the New Testament?

Added books
Why is it in Deuteronomy?

What meaning is there in the Old and New Testament
An oaths must be in the Lord's name.

How many verses in the Old Testament	How many verses in the New Testament
Four.	None.

1240 BC
Deuteronomy ch.10 v20

750 BC
Amos ch.8 v14

720 BC
Hosea ch.4 v15

685 BC
Isaiah ch.48 v1-2

Officers

Most popular Old Testament	Most popular New Testament
2 Kings.	Acts.

If the book is missing, it would be **bold**	
Pentateuch	Gospels
Joshua and Judges	Acts
History books	Letters of Paul
After captivity	**Letter of James**
Psalms	**Letters of Peter**
Proverbs and Ecclesiastes	Pastoral Epistles
Major prophets	**Hebrews**
Minor prophets	**Revelation**

Missing books

Why is it not in the Psalms?

Added books

Why is it in the Pastoral Epistles?

What meaning is there in the Old and New Testament

Officers were appointed to oversee what the king said.

How many verses in the Old Testament	How many verses in the New Testament
Eighty-six.	Nine.

1680 BC
Genesis ch.50 v7

1280 BC
Exodus ch.15 v4

1240 BC
Deuteronomy ch.20 v8; ch.29 v10-12

1220 BC
Joshua ch.1 v10-11; ch.23 v1-2

1010 BC
1 Samuel ch.18 v5; ch.22 v7

975 BC
2 Samuel ch.16 v5-7
1 Chronicles ch.12 v18

630 BC
Nahum ch.2 v5

580 BC
2 Kings ch.5 v13; ch.9 v11; ch.10 v25
2 Chronicles ch.8 v9
Jeremiah ch.26 v21; ch.51 v57

570 BC
Ezekiel ch.23 v12

530 BC
Daniel ch.3 v2

465 BC
Esther ch.8 v9

450 BC
Ezra ch.8 v36

400 BC
Nehemiah ch.2 v9

AD 30
Matthew ch.8 v9
Mark ch.6 v21

AD 63
Acts ch.21 v32; ch.23 v23-24; ch.27 v9

AD 64
Titus ch.3 v1-2

Orphan

Most popular Old Testament	Most popular New Testament
Job.	None.

If the book is missing, it would be **bold**	
	Gospels
Pentateuch	**Acts**
Joshua and Judges	**Letters of Paul**
History books	**Letter of James**
After captivity	**Letters of Peter**
Psalms	**Pastoral Epistles**
Proverbs and Ecclesiastes	**Hebrews**
Major prophets	**Revelation**
Minor prophets	

Missing books
Why is it not in the Major Prophets?

Added books
Why is it in Job?

What meaning is there in the Old and New Testament
An orphan needs some friends.

How many verses in the Old Testament	How many verses in the New Testament
Four.	None.

1300 BC
Job ch.6 v27; ch.31 v21-23

1280 BC
Exodus ch.22 v22-24

1000 BC
Psalm ch.82 v3-4

Palace

Most popular Old Testament	Most popular New Testament
2 Kings.	Luke, Acts and Philippians.

If the book is missing, it would be **bold**	
Pentateuch	Gospels
Joshua and Judges	Acts
History books	Letters of Paul
After captivity	**Letter of James**
Psalms	**Letters of Peter**
Proverbs and Ecclesiastes	**Pastoral Epistles**
Major prophets	**Hebrews**
Minor prophets	**Revelation**

Missing books

Why is it not in Hebrews?

Added books

Why is it in Jeremiah?

What meaning is there in the Old and New Testament

A palace is where the king lives.

How many verses in the Old Testament	How many verses in the New Testament
One hundred and Eighty-six.	Three.

1680 BC
Genesis ch.12 v15; ch.40 v2-3

1280 BC
Exodus ch.7 v23; ch.8 v24

1000 BC
Psalm ch.45 v15

975 BC
2 Samuel ch.5 v11; ch.11 v9; ch.15 v16; ch.16 v22

850 BC
1 Kings ch.7 v1; ch.10 v4-5; ch.20 v6

685 BC
Isaiah ch.32 v14; ch.39 v6-7

630 BC
Nahum ch.2 v6

580 BC
2 Kings ch.11 v5-7; ch.18 v15-16
2 Chronicles ch.12 v9-10
Jeremiah ch.22 v4-5; ch.37 v21; ch.38 v22

530 BC
Daniel ch.4 v29-30

465 BC
Esther ch.1 v5; ch.4 v2-3

AD 30
Luke ch.11 v21-22

AD 53
Philippians ch.1 v13-14

AD 63
Acts ch.7 v10

Pardon

Most popular Old Testament	Most popular New Testament
Numbers and 2 Kings.	None.

If the book is missing, it would be **bold**	
Pentateuch	**Gospels**
Joshua and Judges	**Acts**
History books	**Letters of Paul**
After captivity	**Letter of James**
Psalms	**Letters of Peter**
Proverbs and Ecclesiastes	**Pastoral Epistles**
Major prophets	**Hebrews**
Minor prophets	**Revelation**

Missing books
Why is it not in Ezekiel?

Added books
Why is it in Numbers?

What meaning is there in the Old and New Testament
We need God's pardon for our sins to be forgiven.

How many verses in the Old Testament	How many verses in the New Testament
Nine.	None.

1240 BC
Numbers ch.14 v19-20
Deuteronomy ch.29 v20

580 BC
2 Kings ch.5 v18
2 Chronicles ch.30 v18-20
Jeremiah ch.5 v7-9

550 BC
Joel ch.3 v21

Passion

Most popular Old Testament	Most popular New Testament
Isaiah.	John and 1 Corinthians.

If the book is missing, it would be **bold**	
	Gospels
Pentateuch	**Acts**
Joshua and Judges	Letters of Paul
History books	**Letter of James**
After captivity	**Letters of Peter**
Psalms	**Pastoral Epistles**
Proverbs and Ecclesiastes	**Hebrews**
Major prophets	**Revelation**
Minor prophets	

Missing books

Why is it not in the Pentateuch?

Added books

Why is it in Isaiah?

What meaning is there in the Old and New Testament

Passion is what God commands us to do.

How many verses in the Old Testament	How many verses in the New Testament
Six.	Five.

1000 BC
Psalm ch.69 v9

950 BC
Ecclesiastes ch.7 v26

685 BC
Isaiah ch.57 v5; ch.59 v17; ch.63 v15

515 BC
Zechariah ch.8 v2

AD 30
John ch.1 v13; ch.2 v17

AD 49
1 Thessalonians ch.4 v3-6

AD 53
1 Corinthians ch.7 v36-38

Passover

Most popular Old Testament	Most popular New Testament
2 Chronicles.	John.

If the book is missing, it would be **bold**	
Pentateuch	Gospels
Joshua and Judges	Acts
History books	Letters of Paul
After captivity	**Letter of James**
Psalms	**Letters of Peter**
Proverbs and Ecclesiastes	**Pastoral Epistles**
Major prophets	Hebrews
Minor prophets	**Revelation**

Missing books

Why is it not in the Major and Minor Prophets?

Added books

Why is it in the John's Gospel?

What meaning is there in the Old and New Testament

The Passover was when God spared the Israelites.

How many verses in the Old Testament	How many verses in the New Testament
Seventy-two.	Forty-one.

1240 BC
Numbers ch.9 v13-14
Deuteronomy ch.16 v5-6

1220 BC
Joshua ch.5 v10

580 BC
2 Kings ch.23 v22-23
2 Chronicles ch.30 v4-5

450 BC
Ezra ch.6 v20

AD 30
Matthew ch.27 v15-18
Luke ch.22 v15-16

AD 53
1 Corinthians ch.5 v7-8

AD 63
Acts ch.12 v3-5; ch.20 v6

AD 66
Hebrews ch.11 v28

Perfection

Most popular Old Testament	Most popular New Testament
Psalms.	Philippians and Hebrews.

If the book is missing, it would be **bold**	
	Gospels
Pentateuch	**Acts**
Joshua and Judges	Letters of Paul
History books	**Letter of James**
After captivity	**Letters of Peter**
Psalms	**Pastoral Epistles**
Proverbs and Ecclesiastes	Hebrews
Major prophets	**Revelation**
Minor prophets	

Missing books
Why is it not in the History Books?

Added books
Why is it in Philippians?

What meaning is there in the Old and New Testament
Perfection is the model of brilliance.

How many verses in the Old Testament	How many verses in the New Testament
Four.	Four.

1300 BC
Job ch.37 v16

1000 BC
Psalm ch.50 v2; ch.119 v96

570 BC
Ezekiel ch.28 v12-13

AD 53
Philippians ch.3 v12-13

AD 66
Hebrews ch.7 v11; ch.11 v40

Pit

Most popular Old Testament	Most popular New Testament
Ezekiel.	Revelation.

If the book is missing, it would be **bold**	
	Gospels
Pentateuch	**Acts**
Joshua and Judges	**Letters of Paul**
History books	**Letter of James**
After captivity	**Letters of Peter**
Psalms	**Pastoral Epistles**
Proverbs and Ecclesiastes	**Hebrews**
Major prophets	Revelation
Minor prophets	

Missing books

Why is it not in Joshua and Judges?

Added books

Why is it in Ezekiel?

What meaning is there in the Old and New Testament

A pit is formed by man as a trap and others fall into it.

How many verses in the Old Testament	How many verses in the New Testament
Fifty.	Ten.

1300 BC
Job ch.18 v8

1280 BC
Exodus ch.21 v33-34

1000 BC
Psalm ch.7 v15; ch.9 v15; ch.40 v2; ch.69 v15

975 BC
2 Samuel ch.17 v9-10; ch.18 v17
1 Chronicles ch.11 v22-23

950 BC
Proverbs ch.1 v12

720 BC
Hosea ch.5 v2

685 BC
Isaiah ch.14 v19

580 BC
Jeremiah ch.18 v22

570 BC
Ezekiel ch.26 v20; ch.32 v23

AD 30
Mark ch.12 v1
Luke ch.8 v31; ch.14 v5-6

AD 96
Revelation ch.9 v1-2, v11; ch.20 v1-3

Pity

Most popular Old Testament	Most popular New Testament
Ezekiel.	Matthew and Luke.

If the book is missing, it would be **bold**	
Pentateuch	Gospels
Joshua and Judges	**Acts**
History books	**Letters of Paul**
After captivity	**Letter of James**
Psalms	**Letters of Peter**
Proverbs and Ecclesiastes	**Pastoral Epistles**
Major prophets	**Hebrews**
Minor prophets	**Revelation**

Missing books

Why is it not in Proverbs?

Added books

Why is it in Ezekiel?

What meaning is there in the Old and New Testament

God chooses who will have his pity or who will not.

How many verses in the Old Testament	How many verses in the New Testament
Thirty.	Two.

1300 BC
Job ch.41 v3

1240 BC
Deuteronomy ch.13 v8-9; ch.19 v21; ch.25 v12; ch.28 v50-51

1060 BC
Judges ch.2 v18-19

1000 BC
Psalm ch.17 v10-11; ch.72 v13-14; ch.109 v12-13

975 BC
2 Samuel ch.12 v6

720 BC
Hosea ch.13 v14

685 BC
Isaiah ch.27 v11; ch.51 v3

580 BC
2 Chronicles ch.36 v17-18
Jeremiah ch.21 v7

570 BC
Ezekiel ch.7 v4; ch.8 v18; ch.20 v17; ch.24 v14

550 BC
Joel ch.2 v18

515 BC
Zechariah ch.11 v6

AD 30
Matthew ch.18 v27
Luke ch.16 v24

Plagues

Most popular Old Testament	Most popular New Testament
Deuteronomy and Amos.	Revelation.

If the book is missing, it would be **bold**	
Pentateuch	Gospels
Joshua and Judges	**Acts**
History books	**Letters of Paul**
After captivity	**Letter of James**
Psalms	**Letters of Peter**
Proverbs and Ecclesiastes	**Pastoral Epistles**
Major prophets	**Hebrews**
Minor prophets	Revelation

Missing books
Why is it not in the Major Prophets?

Added books
Why is it in Revelation?

What meaning is there in the Old and New Testament
God sends a plague upon the wicked.

How many verses in the Old Testament	How many verses in the New Testament
Ten.	Eleven.

1680 BC
Genesis ch.12 v17

1280 BC
Exodus ch.9 v14-16

1240 BC
Deuteronomy ch.28 v59

1220 BC
Joshua ch.24 v5

1010 BC
1 Samuel ch.4 v8

750 BC
Amos ch.4 v10

720 BC
Hosea ch.13 v14

580 BC
2 Chronicles ch.7 v13

AD 30
Luke ch.21 v11

AD 96
Revelation ch.9 v18-20; ch.15 v1; ch.16 v9; ch.18 v8; ch.22 v18-19

Plants

Most popular Old Testament	Most popular New Testament
Genesis.	Matthew.

If the book is missing, it would be **bold**	
Pentateuch	Gospels
Joshua and Judges	**Acts**
History books	Letters of Paul
After captivity	**Letter of James**
Psalms	**Letters of Peter**
Proverbs and Ecclesiastes	**Pastoral Epistles**
Major prophets	**Hebrews**
Minor prophets	Revelation

Missing books

Why is it not in Jeremiah and Ezekiel?

Added books

Why is it in 1 and 2 Corinthians?

What meaning is there in the Old and New Testament

God makes the plants and trees to grow.

How many verses in the Old Testament	How many verses in the New Testament
Nineteen.	Fourteen.

1680 BC
Genesis ch.1 v11-12

1300 BC
Job ch.40 v22

1280 BC
Exodus ch.9 v22, v25-26

1240 BC
Deuteronomy ch.32 v2

1000 BC
Psalms ch.104 v14

950 BC
Proverbs ch.16 v28; ch.31 v16

850 BC
1 Kings ch.4 v33

685 BC
Isaiah ch.15 v6; ch.44 v14-15; ch.61 v11

530 BC
Daniel ch.4 v15

AD 30
Matthew ch.13 v6-7, v32, v37-38
Mark ch.4 v14
John ch.4 v37-38

AD 53
1 Corinthians ch.3 v7-9; ch.9 v7-8

AD 55
2 Corinthians ch.9 v6-7

AD 96
Revelation ch.9 v4-5

Poison

Most popular Old Testament	Most popular New Testament
Jeremiah.	James.

If the book is missing, it would be **bold**	
Pentateuch	**Gospels**
Joshua and Judges	**Acts**
History books	**Letters of Paul**
After captivity	Letter of James
Psalms	**Letters of Peter**
Proverbs and Ecclesiastes	**Pastoral Epistles**
Major prophets	**Hebrews**
Minor prophets	**Revelation**

Missing books
Why is it not in Isaiah?

Added books
Why is it in the Letter of James?

What meaning is there in the Old and New Testament
Poison destroys life.

How many verses in the Old Testament	How many verses in the New Testament
Twelve.	One.

1300 BC
Job ch.6 v4; ch.20 v16

1240 BC
Deuteronomy ch.32 v32-33

1000 BC
Psalm ch.69 v21

950 BC
Proverbs ch.5 v4; ch.26 v6

580 BC
2 Kings ch.4 v40
Jeremiah ch.8 v14; ch.9 v15; ch.23 v15

750 BC
Amos ch.6 v12

AD 66
James ch.3 v7-9

Potter

Most popular Old Testament	Most popular New Testament
Isaiah.	Romans.

If the book is missing, it would be **bold**	
	Gospels
Pentateuch	**Acts**
Joshua and Judges	Letters of Paul
History books	**Letter of James**
After captivity	**Letters of Peter**
Psalms	**Pastoral Epistles**
Proverbs and Ecclesiastes	**Hebrews**
Major prophets	**Revelation**
Minor prophets	

Missing books

Why is it not in the History Books?

Added books

Why is it in Zechariah?

What meaning is there in the Old and New Testament

A potter makes a pot out of clay.

How many verses in the Old Testament	How many verses in the New Testament
Ten.	One.

685 BC
Isaiah ch.29 v16; ch.41 v25; ch.64 v8

580 BC
Jeremiah ch.18 v2-7
Lamentations ch.4 v2

515 BC
Zechariah ch.11 v13

AD 55
Romans ch.9 v21-22

Pride

Most popular Old Testament	Most popular New Testament
Isaiah.	1 Corinthians.

If the book is missing, it would be **bold**	
Pentateuch **Joshua and Judges** History books After captivity Psalms Proverbs and Ecclesiastes Major prophets Minor prophets	Gospels **Acts** Letters of Paul **Letter of James** **Letters of Peter** Pastoral Epistles **Hebrews** **Revelation**

Missing books
Why is it not in the Pentateuch?

Added books
Why is it in Isaiah?

What meaning is there in the Old and New Testament
God will judge man's pride.

How many verses in the Old Testament	How many verses in the New Testament
Fifty-seven.	Nine.

1300 BC
Job ch.33 v17; ch.35 v12

1010 BC
1 Samuel ch.17 v28

1000 BC
Psalm ch.59 v12; ch.73 v8-10; ch.101 v5

975 BC
2 Samuel ch.1 v19

950 BC
Proverbs ch.8 v13; ch.11 v2; ch.13 v10; ch.16 v18
Ecclesiastes ch.7 v8

685 BC
Isaiah ch.13 v11; ch.25 v11

580 BC
2 Chronicles ch.32 v26
Jeremiah ch.48 v29-30

570 BC
Ezekiel ch.16 v49-50; ch.28 v17; ch.33 v28
Obadiah ch.1 v3

515 BC
Zechariah ch.9 v6; ch.10 v11

AD 30
Mark ch.7 v20-23

AD 53
1 Corinthians ch.11 v15; ch.15 v31
Philippians ch.1 v26

AD 55
2 Corinthians ch.7 v4

AD 64
2 Timothy ch.3 v4

AD 93
1 John ch.2 v16

Prison

Most popular Old Testament Genesis.	Most popular New Testament Acts.
If the book is missing, it would be **bold** Pentateuch Joshua and Judges History books **After captivity** Psalms Proverbs and Ecclesiastes Major prophets **Minor prophets**	Gospels Acts Letters of Paul **Letter of James** Letters of Peter Pastoral Epistles Hebrews Revelation
Missing books Why is it not in Ezekiel?	
Added books Why is it in Jeremiah?	
What meaning is there in the Old and New Testament Most of his servants remained in prison.	
How many verses in the Old Testament Forty-two.	How many verses in the New Testament Forty-five.

1680 BC
Genesis ch.39 v20-23; ch.40 v15; ch.42 v17-20

1300 BC
Job ch.12 v14

1060 BC
Judges ch.16 v21

1000 BC
Psalm ch.142 v7

950 BC
Ecclesiastes ch.4 v14

850 BC
1 Kings ch.22 v27

685 BC
Isaiah ch.24 v22; ch.42 v7

580 BC
2 Kings ch.25 v29-30
2 Chronicles ch.16 v10
Jeremiah ch.37 v21

AD 30
Matthew ch.5 v25-26; ch.14 v10; ch.18 v34; ch.25 v35-36
Luke ch.22 v33

AD 55
2 Corinthians ch.6 v5-7; ch.11 v23-27

AD 63
Acts ch.8 v3; ch.12 v6-7; ch.16 v23-24, v37

AD 64
2 Timothy ch.1 v8-9, v12

AD 66
Hebrews ch.13 v3

AD 96
Revelation ch.2 v10; ch.13 v10

Prize

Most popular Old Testament Proverbs.	Most popular New Testament 1 Corinthians and 2 Timothy.
If the book is missing, it would be **bold** **Pentateuch** **Joshua and Judges** **History books** **After captivity** **Psalms** Proverbs and Ecclesiastes **Major prophets** **Minor prophets**	**Gospels** **Acts** Letters of Paul **Letter of James** **Letters of Peter** Pastoral Epistles **Hebrews** **Revelation**
Missing books Why is not in the Gospels?	
Added books Why is it in 2 Timothy?	
What meaning is there in the Old and New Testament We should all get a prize at the coming of the Lord Jesus.	
How many verses in the Old Testament One.	How many verses in the New Testament Six.

950 BC
Proverbs ch.4 v8-9

AD 53
1 Corinthians ch.9 v24-26
Philippians ch.3 v14

AD 64
2 Timothy ch.2 v5-7; ch.4 v8

Prophecy

Most popular Old Testament Jeremiah.	Most popular New Testament 1 Corinthians.
If the book is missing, it would be **bold** Pentateuch **Joshua and Judges** History books After captivity **Psalms** **Proverbs and Ecclesiastes** Major prophets Minor prophets	Gospels Acts Letters of Paul **Letter of James** Letters of Peter Pastoral Epistles **Hebrews** Revelation
Missing books Why is it not in Isaiah?	
Added books Why is it in 1 Corinthians?	
What meaning is there in the Old and New Testament A prophecy comes from God, but it will come true.	
How many verses in the Old Testament Twenty.	How many verses in the New Testament Thirty.

1240 BC
Deuteronomy ch.18 v21-22

580 BC
2 Chronicles ch.36 v22
Jeremiah ch.32 v3-4

570 BC
Ezekiel ch.12 v23

530 BC
Daniel ch.12 v4

400 BC
Nehemiah ch.6 v12-13

AD 30
Matthew ch.21 v4-5
Luke ch.1 v67

AD 53
1 Corinthians ch.13 v2-3; ch.14 v4

AD 55
Romans ch.9 v25

AD 63
Acts ch.21 v9

AD 64
1 Timothy ch.4 v14-15

AD 80
2 Peter ch.1 v20-21

AD 96
Revelation ch.19 v10; ch.22 v18-19

Proverb

Most popular Old Testament	Most popular New Testament
Ezekiel.	Luke and 2 Peter.

If the book is missing, it would be **bold**	
Pentateuch	Gospels
Joshua and Judges	**Acts**
History books	**Letters of Paul**
After captivity	**Letter of James**
Psalms	Letters of Peter
Proverbs and Ecclesiastes	**Pastoral Epistles**
Major prophets	**Hebrews**
Minor prophets	**Revelation**

Missing books	
Why is it not in Isaiah?	

Added books
Why is it in 2 Peter?

What meaning is there in the Old and New Testament
A proverb is like a morale lesson.

How many verses in the Old Testament	How many verses in the New Testament
Eleven.	Two.

1680 BC
Genesis ch.22 v14

1010 BC
1 Samuel ch.24 v13-15

950 BC
Proverbs ch.26 v7-9

580 BC
Jeremiah ch.31 v29-30

570 BC
Ezekiel ch.12 v21-23; ch.18 v1-4

AD 30
Luke ch.4 v23-24

AD 80
2 Peter ch.2 v22

Punishment

Most popular Old Testament	Most popular New Testament
Jeremiah.	Romans.

If the book is missing, it would be **bold**	
Pentateuch	Gospels
Joshua and Judges	Acts
History books	Letters of Paul
After captivity	**Letter of James**
Psalms	Letters of Peter
Proverbs and Ecclesiastes	**Pastoral Epistles**
Major prophets	Hebrews
Minor prophets	**Revelation**

Missing books

Why is it not in Luke's Gospel?

Added books

Why is it in Hosea?

What meaning is there in the Old and New Testament

God who will give just punishment.

How many verses in the Old Testament	How many verses in the New Testament
Sixty-three.	Twelve.

1680 BC
Genesis ch.4 v13-14

1300 BC
Job ch.8 v4; ch.19 v20

1280 BC
Exodus ch.21 v23-25

1240 BC
Numbers ch.15 v31

1000 BC
Psalm ch.10 v5; ch.149 v7

950 BC
Proverbs ch.20 v30

750 BC
Amos ch.8 v2-3

720 BC
Hosea ch.9 v7

690 BC
Micah ch.7 v4

685 BC
Isaiah ch.1 v5; ch.53 v4; ch.66 v15-16

580 BC
Jeremiah ch.4 v18; ch.16 v17; ch.51 v56

570 BC
Ezekiel ch.16 v58; ch.23 v24-27

AD 30
Matthew ch.5 v38-39; ch.25 v46

AD 55
Romans ch.2 v5-7; ch.4 v15; ch.13 v5
2 Corinthians ch.2 v6-8; ch.11 v15

AD 63
Acts ch.13 v11

AD 66
Hebrews ch.10 v29

AD 80
2 Peter ch.2 v9-10

AD 93
1 John ch.4 v18-19

Purity

Most popular Old Testament	Most popular New Testament
Proverbs.	1 Timothy.

If the book is missing, it would be **bold**	
Pentateuch	Gospels
Joshua and Judges	**Acts**
History books	Letters of Paul
After captivity	**Letter of James**
Psalms	**Letters of Peter**
Proverbs and Ecclesiastes	Pastoral Epistles
Major prophets	**Hebrews**
Minor prophets	**Revelation**

Missing books

Why is it not in the Major Prophets?

Added books

Why is it in 1 Timothy?

What meaning is there in the Old and New Testament

We prove ourselves by our purity.

How many verses in the Old Testament	How many verses in the New Testament
Six.	Five.

1300 BC
Job ch.14 v4

1000 BC
Psalm ch.86 v11

950 BC
Proverbs ch.17 v3; ch.27 v21

AD 55
2 Corinthians ch.6 v6-7

AD 64
1 Timothy ch.4 v12-13; ch.5 v2

Quarry

Most popular Old Testament	Most popular New Testament
1 Kings and 2 Chronicles.	None.

If the book is missing, it would be **bold**	
	Gospels
Pentateuch	**Acts**
Joshua and Judges	**Letters of Paul**
History books	**Letter of James**
After captivity	**Letters of Peter**
Psalms	**Pastoral Epistles**
Proverbs and Ecclesiastes	**Hebrews**
Major prophets	**Revelation**
Minor prophets	

Missing books
Why is it not in the Minor Prophets?

Added books
Why is it in Isaiah?

What meaning is there in the Old and New Testament
If you work in a quarry, stones might fall and crush you.

How many verses in the Old Testament	How many verses in the New Testament
Six.	None.

950 BC
Ecclesiastes ch.10 v9

850 BC
1 Kings ch.5 v15-16; ch.6 v7

685 BC
Isaiah ch.51 v1

580 BC
2 Chronicles ch.2 v2, v18

Rain

Most popular Old Testament	Most popular New Testament
Job.	Matthew and the Letter of James.

If the book is missing, it would be **bold**	
	Gospels
Pentateuch	Acts
Joshua and Judges	**Letters of Paul**
History books	Letter of James
After captivity	**Letters of Peter**
Psalms	**Pastoral Epistles**
Proverbs and Ecclesiastes	Hebrews
Major prophets	Revelation
Minor prophets	

Missing books

Why is it not in the Letters of Paul?

Added books

Why is it in Psalms?

What meaning is there in the Old and New Testament

God gives rain to produce and let plants grow.

How many verses in the Old Testament	How many verses in the New Testament
Ninety-three.	Eight.

1680 BC
Genesis ch.2 v5; ch.7 v11-12

1300 BC
Job ch.5 v10; ch.28 v25-26

1280 BC
Exodus ch.9 v34; ch.16 v4

1240 BC
Deuteronomy ch.11 v11-12; ch.28 v12; ch.32 v2

1010 BC
1 Samuel ch.12 v16-17

1000 BC
Psalm ch.68 v9

975 BC
2 Samuel ch.22 v12

950 BC
Proverbs ch.25 v14; ch.28 v3

850 BC
1 Kings ch.8 v35; ch.17 v1

750 BC
Amos ch.4 v7

690 BC
Micah ch.5 v7

685 BC
Isaiah ch.5 v6; ch.55 v10

580 BC
Jeremiah ch.10 v13

570 BC
Ezekiel ch.38 v22-23

AD 30
Matthew ch.5 v45

AD 63
Acts ch.14 v17

AD 66
Hebrews ch.6 v7-8
James ch.5 v18

AD 80
Jude ch.1 v12-13

AD 96
Revelation ch.11 v6

Refuge

Most popular Old Testament	Most popular New Testament
Psalms.	Hebrews.

If the book is missing, it would be **bold**	
	Gospels
Pentateuch	**Acts**
Joshua and Judges	**Letters of Paul**
History books	**Letter of James**
After captivity	**Letters of Peter**
Psalms	**Pastoral Epistles**
Proverbs and Ecclesiastes	Hebrews
Major prophets	**Revelation**
Minor prophets	

Missing books
Why is it not in Ezekiel?

Added books
Why is it in Joshua?

What meaning is there in the Old and New Testament
God is our refuge and his everlasting arms are under you.

How many verses in the Old Testament	How many verses in the New Testament
Fifty-one.	One.

1280 BC
Exodus ch.21 v13

1240 BC
Numbers ch.35 v28-29
Deuteronomy ch.23 v15-16; ch.33 v27

1000 BC
Psalm ch.9 v9; ch.91 v9-11

950 BC
Proverbs ch.14 v26

685 BC
Isaiah ch.25 v4; ch.28 v17

580 BC
Jeremiah ch.16 v19

550 BC
Joel ch.3 v16

AD 66
Hebrews ch.6 v18-19

Repentance

Most popular Old Testament	Most popular New Testament
2 Chronicles.	Hebrews.

If the book is missing, it would be **bold**	
Pentateuch	Gospels
Joshua and Judges	Acts
History books	Letters of Paul
After captivity	**Letter of James**
Psalms	**Letters of Peter**
Proverbs and Ecclesiastes	**Pastoral Epistles**
Major prophets	Hebrews
Minor prophets	**Revelation**

Missing books
Why is it not in the Psalms or Revelation?

Added books
Why is it in 2 Chronicles?

What meaning is there in the Old and New Testament
Repentance is failing to do what God commanded.

How many verses in the Old Testament	How many verses in the New Testament
Eleven.	Eight.

1300 BC
Job ch.42 v6

850 BC
1 Kings ch.8 v47

580 BC
2 Kings ch.22 v19
Jeremiah ch.36 v24

AD 30
Luke ch.17 v3-4

AD 63
Acts ch.19 v4

AD 55
2 Corinthians ch.7 v10

AD 66
Hebrews ch.6 v4-6; ch.12 v17

Resurrection

Most popular Old Testament	Most popular New Testament
None.	1 Corinthians.

If the book is missing, it would be **bold**	
Pentateuch	Gospels
Joshua and Judges	Acts
History books	Letters of Paul
After captivity	**Letter of James**
Psalms	Letters of Peter
Proverbs and Ecclesiastes	Pastoral Epistles
Major prophets	Hebrews
Minor prophets	Revelation

Missing books
Why is it not in the Letter of James?

Added books
Why is it in 1 Corinthians?

What meaning is there in the Old and New Testament
God will also resurrect our earthly bodies.

How many verses in the Old Testament	How many verses in the New Testament
None.	Forty-seven.

AD 30
Matthew ch.22 v31-32
Luke ch.14 v14
John ch.11 v25

AD 53
1 Corinthians ch.15 v12, v23, v42
Philippians ch.3 v11

AD 63
Acts ch.2 v31; ch.4 v2; ch.17 v32; ch.23 v7

AD 64
1 Peter ch.3 v21

AD 66
Hebrews ch.6 v2; ch.11 v35-38

AD 96
Revelation ch.20 v5-6

Righteousness

Most popular Old Testament	Most popular New Testament
Isaiah.	Matthew, Romans and 2 Corinthians.

If the book is missing, it would be **bold**	
Pentateuch	Gospels
Joshua and Judges	Acts
History books	Letters of Paul
After captivity	Letter of James
Psalms	Letters of Peter
Proverbs and Ecclesiastes	Pastoral Epistles
Major prophets	Hebrews
Minor prophets	**Revelation**

Missing books

Why is it not in Mark's Gospel?

Added books

Why is it in Isaiah?

What meaning is there in the Old and New Testament

God is righteous and he maintains justice.

How many verses in the Old Testament	How many verses in the New Testament
Sixty-three.	Twenty-six.

1300 BC
Job ch.29 v14

1000 BC
Psalm ch.71 v19; ch.89 v14; ch.99 v4

950 BC
Proverbs ch.21 v21

850 BC
1 Kings ch.10 v9

720 BC
Hosea ch.10 v12

690 BC
Micah ch.7 v9

685 BC
Isaiah ch.5 v7; ch.28 v17; ch.45 v24

580 BC
Jeremiah ch.4 v2

570 BC
Ezekiel ch.22 v30-31

AD 30
Matthew ch.5 v20
John ch.16 v8-11

AD 53
Philippians ch.3 v9

AD 54
Galatians ch.5 v5

AD 55
Romans ch.5 v17
2 Corinthians ch.6 v7-8

AD 63
Acts ch.24 v25

AD 64
1 Timothy ch.6 v11
Titus ch.2 v12

AD 66
James ch.3 v18

AD 80
2 Peter ch.3 v13

Rock

Most popular Old Testament Psalms.	Most popular New Testament Matthew.
If the book is missing, it would be **bold** Pentateuch Joshua and Judges History books After captivity Psalms Proverbs and Ecclesiastes Major prophets Minor prophets	Gospels **Acts** Letters of Paul **Letter of James** Letters of Peter **Pastoral Epistles** **Hebrews** **Revelation**

Missing books Why is it not in Acts?

Added books Why is it in Matthew's Gospel?

What meaning is there in the Old and New Testament Rock means a mass of stone and God is the rock.

How many verses in the Old Testament One hundred and Three.	How many verses in the New Testament Fourteen.

1300 BC
Job ch.28 v2

1280 BC
Exodus ch.22 v21-23

1240 BC
Numbers ch.20 v10-11
Deuteronomy ch.32 v4, v18

1060 BC
Judges ch.6 v21; ch.20 v16-17

1010 BC
1 Samuel ch.2 v2

1000 BC
Psalm ch.31 v3; ch.71 v3; ch.92 v15

975 BC
2 Samuel ch.22 v32

685 BC
Isaiah ch.17 v10

620 BC
Habakkuk ch.1 v12

580 BC
Jeremiah ch.49 v16

570 BC
Ezekiel ch.26 v4-5

515 BC
Zechariah ch.12 v3

AD 30
Matthew ch.7 v24; ch.16 v18
Mark ch.15 v46-47

AD 53
1 Corinthians ch.10 v4-5

AD 55
Romans ch.9 v32-33

AD 64
1 Peter ch.2 v8

Rule

Most popular Old Testament 2 Kings.	Most popular New Testament Revelation.
If the book is missing, it would be **bold** Pentateuch Joshua and Judges History books After captivity Psalms Proverbs and Ecclesiastes Major prophets Minor prophets	Gospels Acts Letters of Paul **Letter of James** **Letters of Peter** **Pastoral Epistles** Hebrews Revelation
Missing books Why is it not in Exodus?	
Added books Why is it in 1 and 2 Kings?	
What meaning is there in the Old and New Testament A rule is a direction or instruction.	
How many verses in the Old Testament One hundred and Twenty-one.	How many verses in the New Testament Eleven.

1680 BC
Genesis ch.3 v16

1240 BC
Leviticus ch.26 v17
Deuteronomy ch.15 v6

1010 BC
1 Samuel ch.9 v17

975 BC
2 Samuel ch.3 v21

950 BC
Proverbs ch.22 v7

690 BC
Micah ch.4 v7

685 BC
Isaiah ch.14 v2; ch.32 v1

580 BC
Jeremiah ch.5 v31

570 BC
Ezekiel ch.18 v4

530 BC
Daniel ch.6 v26

515 BC
Zechariah ch.6 v13

AD 53
1 Corinthians ch.7 v17-18

AD 55
Romans ch.5 v17

AD 61
Colossians ch.3 v15

AD 63
Acts ch.13 v20-21

AD 66
Hebrews ch.1 v8-9

AD 96
Revelation ch.19 v15-16

Salvation

Most popular Old Testament Isaiah.	Most popular New Testament Romans.
If the book is missing, it would be **bold** Pentateuch **Joshua and Judges** History books **After captivity** Psalms **Proverbs and Ecclesiastes** Major prophets Minor prophets	Gospels Acts Letters of Paul **Letter of James** Letters of Peter Pastoral Epistles Hebrews Revelation

Missing books Why is it not in Matthew's Gospel?
Added books Why is it in Psalms?
What meaning is there in the Old and New Testament Salvation comes from God alone.

How many verses in the Old Testament Fifty-eight.	How many verses in the New Testament Fifty-six.

1680 BC
Genesis ch.49 v18

1000 BC
Psalm ch.27 v1; ch.51 v2; ch.74 v12; ch.91 v16; ch.103 v17-18

975 BC
2 Samuel ch.22 v47

750 BC
Jonah ch.2 v9

685 BC
Isaiah ch.25 v9; ch.33 v6; ch.58 v8

620 BC
Habakkuk ch.3 v18

580 BC
2 Chronicles ch.6 v41
Jeremiah ch.3 v23

AD 30
Luke ch.1 v77; ch.19 v9-10; ch.21 v28

AD 50
2 Thessalonians ch.2 v13-14

AD 53
Philippians ch.1 v11; ch.2 v12-13

AD 54
Galatians ch.5 v11-12

AD 55
Romans ch.11 v15; ch.13 v11-12
2 Corinthians ch.6 v2

AD 61
Ephesians ch.2 v9-10

AD 63
Acts ch.4 v12; ch.28 v28

AD 64
2 Timothy ch.3 v15-16
1 Peter ch.1 v10-11, v13-14

AD 66
Hebrews ch.5 v9-10

AD 80
Jude ch.1 v3

AD 96
Revelation ch.12 v10

Sand

Most popular Old Testament	Most popular New Testament
Genesis, Psalms, Isaiah and Jeremiah.	Matthew, Romans, Hebrews and Revelation.
If the book is missing, it would be **bold** Pentateuch Joshua and Judges History books **After captivity** Psalms Proverbs and Ecclesiastes Major prophets Minor prophets	Gospels **Acts** Letters of Paul **Letter of James** **Letters of Peter** **Pastoral Epistles** Hebrews Revelation

Missing books
Why is it not in Ezekiel?

Added books
Why is it in Habbakuk?

What meaning is there in the Old and New Testament
A quantity of sand is too much to count.

How many verses in the Old Testament	How many verses in the New Testament
Eighteen.	Four.

1680 BC
Genesis ch.22 v17; ch.41 v49

1240 BC
Deuteronomy ch.33 v19

1220 BC
Joshua ch.11 v4

1060 BC
Judges ch.7 v12

1010 BC
1 Samuel ch.13 v5

1000 BC
Psalm ch.78 v27; ch.139 v18

975 BC
2 Samuel ch.17 v11

950 BC
Proverbs ch.27 v3

850 BC
1 Kings ch.4 v20

685 BC
Isaiah ch.10 v22; ch.40 v15

620 BC
Habakkuk ch.1 v9

580 BC
Jeremiah ch.15 v8; ch.33 v22

AD 30
Matthew ch.7 v26-27

AD 55
Romans ch.9 v27-28

AD 66
Hebrews ch.11 v12

AD 96
Revelation ch.20 v8-9

Seed

Most popular Old Testament Leviticus.	Most popular New Testament Mark.
If the book is missing, it would be **bold** Pentateuch **Joshua and Judges** **History books** After captivity Psalms Proverbs and Ecclesiastes Major prophets Minor prophets	Gospels **Acts** Letters of Paul **Letter of James** **Letters of Peter** **Pastoral Epistles** Hebrews **Revelation**

Missing books Why is it not in the History Books?
Added books Why is it in Leviticus?
What meaning is there in the Old and New Testament The seeds can be planted in the fields.

How many verses in the Old Testament Twenty.	How many verses in the New Testament Forty-eight.

1680 BC
Genesis ch.47 v23-24

1280 BC
Exodus ch.16 v31

1240 BC
Leviticus ch.11 v37-38; ch.19 v19
Deuteronomy ch.11 v10

1000 BC
Psalm ch.126 v6
Ecclesiastes ch.11 v6

685 BC
Isaiah ch.32 v20; ch.55 v10

580 BC
Jeremiah ch.4 v3

570 BC
Ezekiel ch.17 v23

515 BC
Haggai ch.2 v19

AD 30
Matthew ch.13 v23-24, v37-38; ch.17 v20

AD 53
1 Corinthians ch.3 v6-8; ch.9 v11; ch.15 v36-39

AD 55
2 Corinthians ch.9 v10

AD 66
Hebrews ch.7 v10

Serpent

Most popular Old Testament	Most popular New Testament
Genesis.	Revelation.

If the book is missing, it would be **bold**	
Pentateuch	**Gospels**
Joshua and Judges	**Acts**
History books	Letters of Paul
After captivity	**Letter of James**
Psalms	**Letters of Peter**
Proverbs and Ecclesiastes	**Pastoral Epistles**
Major prophets	**Hebrews**
Minor prophets	Revelation

Missing books

Why is it not in the Psalms?

Added books

Why is it in Revelation?

What meaning is there in the Old and New Testament

A serpent is a poisonous snake.

How many verses in the Old Testament	How many verses in the New Testament
Fifteen.	Three.

1680 BC
Genesis ch.3 v1, v13

1300 BC
Job ch.26 v13

1280 BC
Exodus ch.7 v9

750 BC
Amos ch.9 v3

685 BC
Isaiah ch.14 v29; ch.27 v1

580 BC
2 Kings ch.18 v4
Jeremiah ch.46 v22

AD 55
2 Corinthians ch.11 v3

AD 96
Revelation ch.12 v9; ch.20 v2-3

Shadow

Most popular Old Testament Psalms.	Most popular New Testament Hebrews.
If the book is missing, it would be **bold** **Pentateuch** **Joshua and Judges** History books **After captivity** Psalms Proverbs and Ecclesiastes Major prophets **Minor prophets**	Gospels Acts **Letters of Paul** Letter of James **Letters of Peter** **Pastoral Epistles** Hebrews **Revelation**
Missing books Why is it not in the Letters of Paul?	
Added books Why is it in Isaiah?	
What meaning is there in the Old and New Testament Man's days are like a shadow.	
How many verses in the Old Testament Twenty-five.	How many verses in the New Testament Six.

1300 BC
Job ch.8 v9; ch.17 v7

1000 BC
Psalm ch.17 v8; ch.57 v1; ch.91 v1; ch.144 v4

950 BC
Ecclesiastes ch.6 v12

975 BC
1 Chronicles ch.29 v15

685 BC
Isaiah ch.25 v7-8; ch.49 v2

580 BC
2 Kings ch.20 v10
Lamentations ch.4 v20

570 BC
Ezekiel ch.31 v12

AD 30
Matthew ch.4 v16
Luke ch.1 v79

AD 63
Acts ch.5 v15-16

AD 66
Hebrews ch.8 v5; ch.10 v1-2
James ch.1 v17

Shepherd

Most popular Old Testament	Most popular New Testament
Zechariah.	John's Gospel.

If the book is missing, it would be **bold**	
Pentateuch	Gospels
Joshua and Judges	Acts
History books	Letters of Paul
After captivity	**Letter of James**
Psalms	Letters of Peter
Proverbs and Ecclesiastes	**Pastoral Epistles**
Major prophets	Hebrews
Minor prophets	Revelation

Missing books

Why is it not in Luke's Gospel?

Added books

Why is it in Zechariah?

What meaning is there in the Old and New Testament

God will be our shepherd looking after his sheep.

How many verses in the Old Testament	How many verses in the New Testament
Forty-three.	Nineteen.

1680 BC
Genesis ch.49 v24

1240 BC
Numbers ch.27 v17

1010 BC
1 Samuel ch.17 v20

1000 BC
Psalm ch.23 v1

975 BC
2 Samuel ch.5 v2

950 BC
Ecclesiastes ch.12 v11

750 BC
Amos ch.3 v12

685 BC
Isaiah ch.40 v11

580 BC
2 Chronicles ch.18 v16
Jeremiah ch.31 v10

570 BC
Ezekiel ch.34 v12-14

515 BC
Zechariah ch.10 v2

AD 30
Matthew ch.2 v6; ch.25 v32-33
Mark ch.14 v27
John ch.10 v2-5, v24

AD 53
1 Corinthians ch.9 v7-8

AD 63
Acts ch.20 v28

AD 64
1 Peter ch.2 v25; ch.5 v4

AD 66
Hebrews ch.13 v20

AD 96
Revelation ch.7 v17

Sickness

Most popular Old Testament	Most popular New Testament
Deuteronomy, Isaiah and Jeremiah.	Matthew, Luke, John and Acts.

If the book is missing, it would be **bold**	
Pentateuch	Gospels
Joshua and Judges	Acts
History books	**Letters of Paul**
After captivity	**Letter of James**
Psalms	**Letters of Peter**
Proverbs and Ecclesiastes	**Pastoral Epistles**
Major prophets	**Hebrews**
Minor prophets	**Revelation**

Missing books
Why is it not in Mark's Gospel?

Added books
Why is it in the Exodus?

What meaning is there in the Old and New Testament
The Lord will protect you from sickness.

How many verses in the Old Testament	How many verses in the New Testament
Ten.	Four.

1240 BC
Deuteronomy ch.7 v15; ch.28 v61-62

685 BC
Isaiah ch.38 v15

580 BC
Jeremiah ch.6 v7; ch.10 v19
Lamentations ch.1 v13

570 BC
Ezekiel ch.4 v14

AD 30
Matthew ch.4 v24-25
Luke ch.13 v12-13
John ch.11 v4

AD 63
Acts ch.12 v23

Sign

Most popular Old Testament Exodus and Isaiah.	Most popular New Testament Matthew.
If the book is missing, it would be **bold** Pentateuch Joshua and Judges History books After captivity Psalms **Proverbs and Ecclesiastes** Major prophets Minor prophets	Gospels Acts Letters of Paul **Letter of James** **Letters of Peter** **Pastoral Epistles** **Hebrews** **Revelation**

Missing books Why is it not in Jeremiah?
Added books Why is it in Matthew's Gospel?
What meaning is there in the Old and New Testament There were a lot of signs.

How many verses in the Old Testament Forty-seven.	How many verses in the New Testament Forty-four.

1680 BC
Genesis ch.9 v13; ch.17 v11

1280 BC
Exodus ch.3 v12; ch.13 v9; ch.31 v17

1240 BC
Deuteronomy ch.28 v46

1010 BC
1 Samuel ch.1 v11; ch.14 v10

975 BC
2 Samuel ch.15 v30

850 BC
1 Kings ch.13 v3

685 BC
Isaiah ch.7 v14; ch.55 v13

580 BC
2 Kings ch.20 v9

570 BC
Ezekiel ch.12 v6

AD 30
Matthew ch.12 v38; ch.24 v3
Luke ch.2 v12
John ch.6 v14

AD 53
1 Corinthians ch.14 v22
Philippians ch.1 v28

AD 63
Acts ch.4 v16; ch.13 v51

Singers

Most popular Old Testament	Most popular New Testament
Nehemiah.	Revelation.

If the book is missing, it would be **bold**	
	Gospels
Pentateuch	**Acts**
Joshua and Judges	**Letters of Paul**
History books	**Letter of James**
After captivity	**Letters of Peter**
Psalms	**Pastoral Epistles**
Proverbs and Ecclesiastes	**Hebrews**
Major prophets	Revelation
Minor prophets	

Missing books

Why is it not in the Major and Minor Prophets?

Added books

Why is it in Nehemiah?

What meaning is there in the Old and New Testament

Singers were appointed to sing and make music.

How many verses in the Old Testament	How many verses in the New Testament
Twenty-seven.	One.

1000 BC
Psalm ch.68 v25

975 BC
2 Samuel ch.19 v35
1 Chronicles ch.15 v16

950 BC
Ecclesiastes ch.2 v8

580 BC
2 Chronicles ch.20 v21; ch.29 v28

450 BC
Ezra ch.2 v65

400 BC
Nehemiah ch.7 v1; ch.12 v29, v45-47; ch.13 v10-11

AD 96
Revelation ch.18 v22

Sleep

Most popular Old Testament	Most popular New Testament
Genesis.	Matthew, Mark, Romans and 1 Thessalonians.
If the book is missing, it would be **bold** Pentateuch Joshua and Judges History books After captivity Psalms Proverbs and Ecclesiastes Major prophets Minor prophets	Gospels **Acts** Letters of Paul **Letter of James** **Letters of Peter** **Pastoral Epistles** **Hebrews** **Revelation**
Missing books Why is it not in Revelation?	
Added books Why is it in Genesis?	
What meaning is there in the Old and New Testament Sleep is when you rest after your day's work.	
How many verses in the Old Testament Fifty-eight.	How many verses in the New Testament Four.

1680 BC
Genesis ch.2 v21-22; ch.15 v12-14; ch.28 v16-17; ch.39 v10-11

1300 BC
Job ch.4 v13; ch.33 v15-18

1280 BC
Exodus ch.22 v27

1240 BC
Leviticus ch.26 v6
Deuteronomy ch.28 v30

1010 BC
1 Samuel ch.26 v12

1000 BC
Psalm ch.59 v15

975 BC
2 Samuel ch.16 v21

950 BC
Proverbs ch.3 v24; ch.6 v10-11
Ecclesiastes ch.5 v12

750 BC
Amos ch.2 v7
Jonah ch.1 v6

685 BC
Isaiah ch.26 v19; ch.29 v10

570 BC
Ezekiel ch.34 v25

530 BC
Daniel ch.6 v18

AD 30
Matthew ch.26 v45-46

AD 49
1 Thessalonians ch.5 v7-8

AD 55
Romans ch.11 v8

Snow

Most popular Old Testament Job.	Most popular New Testament Matthew and Revelation.
If the book is missing, it would be **bold** Pentateuch **Joshua and Judges** History books After captivity Psalms Proverbs and Ecclesiastes Major prophets Minor prophets	Gospels **Acts** **Letters of Paul** **Letter of James** **Letters of Peter** **Pastoral Epistles** **Hebrews** Revelation
Missing books Why is it not in Ezekiel?	
Added books Why is it in Job?	
What meaning is there in the Old and New Testament God directs the snow and rain.	
How many verses in the Old Testament Seventeen.	How many verses in the New Testament Two.

1300 BC
Job ch.6 v15; ch.24 v19; ch.37 v6; ch.38 v22

1280 BC
Exodus ch.4 v6-7

1240 BC
Numbers ch.12 v9-10

1000 BC
Psalm ch.51 v7; ch.147 v16; ch.148 v8

950 BC
Proverbs ch.25 v13; ch.26 v1

685 BC
Isaiah ch.1 v18; ch.55 v10

580 BC
2 Kings ch.5 v27
Jeremiah ch.18 v14
Lamentations ch.4 v7

530 BC
Daniel ch.7 v9

AD 30
Matthew ch.28 v3-4

AD 96
Revelation ch.1 v14

Soldier

Most popular Old Testament	Most popular New Testament
1 Kings, 2 Chronicles and Isaiah.	Acts and 2 Timothy.

If the book is missing, it would be **bold**	
Pentateuch	Gospels
Joshua and Judges	Acts
History books	Letters of Paul
After captivity	**Letter of James**
Psalms	**Letters of Peter**
Proverbs and Ecclesiastes	Pastoral Epistles
Major prophets	**Hebrews**
Minor prophets	**Revelation**

Missing books

Why is it not in Jeremiah?

Added books

Why is it in the Pastoral Epistles?

What meaning is there in the Old and New Testament

A soldier is expected to fight.

How many verses in the Old Testament	How many verses in the New Testament
Six.	Nine.

850 BC
1 Kings ch.20 v20

685 BC
Isaiah ch.14 v31; ch.53 v12

580 BC
2 Chronicles ch.17 v17-18; ch.18 v33

AD 30
Matthew ch.5 v41
Mark ch.6 v27

AD 53
1 Corinthians ch.9 v7
Philippians ch.2 v25-26

AD 61
Philemon ch.1 v1-2

AD 63
Acts ch.10 v7-8; ch.28 v16

AD 64
2 Timothy ch.2 v3-5

Soul

Most popular Old Testament	Most popular New Testament
Psalms.	Matthew.

If the book is missing, it would be **bold**	
	Gospels
Pentateuch	Acts
Joshua and Judges	Letters of Paul
History books	**Letter of James**
After captivity	Letters of Peter
Psalms	**Pastoral Epistles**
Proverbs and Ecclesiastes	Hebrews
Major prophets	**Revelation**
Minor prophets	

Missing books

Why is it not in the Isaiah and Jeremiah?

Added books

Why is it in Deuteronomy?

What meaning is there in the Old and New Testament

A soul thinks, feels and desires as distinct from the body.

How many verses in the Old Testament	How many verses in the New Testament
Forty-one.	Twenty.

1300 BC
Job ch.27 v2-4

1240 BC
Deuteronomy ch.4 v29; ch.28 v65-67

1220 BC
Joshua ch.22 v5

1000 BC
Psalm ch.84 v2

950 BC
Proverbs ch.24 v12

850 BC
1 Kings ch.2 v4

580 BC
2 Kings ch.23 v25

570 BC
Ezekiel ch.29 v11-12

AD 30
Matthew ch.10 v28; ch.16 v26; ch.23 v37-40
Luke ch.16 v22-23
John ch.12 v27-28

AD 49
1 Thessalonians ch.5 v23

AD 63
Acts ch.2 v27

AD 66
Hebrews ch.4 v12-13

AD 80
2 Peter ch.2 v8

Stars

Most popular Old Testament	Most popular New Testament
Job.	Revelation.
If the book is missing, it would be **bold** Pentateuch Joshua and Judges History books After captivity Psalms Proverbs and Ecclesiastes Major prophets Minor prophets	Gospels Acts Letters of Paul **Letter of James** **Letters of Peter** **Pastoral Epistles** Hebrews Revelation

Missing books
Why is it not in Proverbs?

Added books
Why it in Job?

What meaning is there in the Old and New Testament
God made the stars and he calls each one by name.

How many verses in the Old Testament	How many verses in the New Testament
Forty-nine.	Eighteen.

1680 BC
Genesis ch.1 v16-18; ch.15 v5

1300 BC
Job ch.9 v9-10

1240 BC
Deuteronomy ch.28 v62

1000 BC
Psalm ch.8 v3; ch.147 v4-5

750 BC
Amos ch.5 v8

685 BC
Isaiah ch.14 v13; ch.40 v26; ch.45 v12

580 BC
Jeremiah ch.31 v35; ch.33 v22

570 BC
Ezekiel ch.32 v8
Obadiah ch.1 v4

530 BC
Daniel ch.12 v3-4

AD 30
Matthew ch.24 v29

AD 53
1 Corinthians ch.15 v41

AD 66
Hebrews ch.11 v12

AD 80
Jude ch.1 v13

AD 96
Revelation ch.6 v13-14

Suffering

Most popular Old Testament	Most popular New Testament
Psalms and Isaiah.	1 Peter.

If the book is missing, it would be **bold**	
Pentateuch Joshua and Judges History books After captivity Psalms **Proverbs and Ecclesiastes** Major prophets Minor prophets	Gospels Acts Letters of Paul Letter of James Letters of Peter Pastoral Epistles Hebrews Revelation

Missing books
Why is it not in Genesis or Ezekiel?

Added books
Why is it in 1 Peter?

What meaning is there in the Old and New Testament
Suffering is needed because the world hates God.

How many verses in the Old Testament	How many verses in the New Testament
Thirty-seven.	Forty-four.

1300 BC
Job ch.30 v27

1280 BC
Exodus ch.3 v7-8

1240 BC
Numbers ch.14 v34
Deuteronomy ch.4 v30-31

1060 BC
Judges ch.2 v18-19

1000 BC
Psalm ch.44 v24; ch.119 v71

685 BC
Isaiah ch.30 v20; ch.61 v8

580 BC
Jeremiah ch.15 v18

570 BC
Obadiah ch.1 v13

515 BC
Zechariah ch.11 v11

AD 30
Matthew ch.26 v39
Luke ch.12 v50-51

AD 49
1 Thessalonians ch.1 v6

AD 50
2 Thessalonians ch.1 v5-6

AD 53
Philippians ch.1 v29-30

AD 55
Romans ch.8 v17
2 Corinthians ch.4 v10

AD 63
Acts ch.20 v23-24

AD 64
2 Timothy ch.4 v5
1 Peter ch.2 v21; ch.5 v9

AD 66
Hebrews ch.2 v18; ch.10 v32-34
James ch.5 v13

AD 96
Revelation ch.2 v9

Symbol

Most popular Old Testament Isaiah.	Most popular New Testament Romans.
If the book is missing, it would be **bold** Pentateuch **Joshua and Judges** History books After captivity Psalms **Proverbs and Ecclesiastes** Major prophets Minor prophets	**Gospels** **Acts** Letters of Paul **Letter of James** **Letters of Peter** **Pastoral Epistles** **Hebrews** **Revelation**
Missing books Why is it not in Hebrews?	
Added books Why is it in Isaiah?	
What meaning is there in the Old and New Testament A symbol is what God can do for you.	
How many verses in the Old Testament Eight.	How many verses in the New Testament One.

1240 BC
Numbers ch.6 v7-8

1000 BC
Psalm ch.132 v8

685 BC
Isaiah ch.20 v3; ch.42 v6

580 BC
2 Chronicles ch.6 v41
Jeremiah ch.24 v9-10

570 BC
Ezekiel ch.24 v27

515 BC
Zechariah ch.8 v13

AD 55
Romans ch.5 v14-16

Table

Most popular Old Testament Exodus.	Most popular New Testament Luke.
If the book is missing, it would be **bold** Pentateuch Joshua and Judges History books After captivity Psalms Proverbs and Ecclesiastes Major prophets Minor prophets	Gospels **Acts** Letters of Paul **Letter of James** **Letters of Peter** **Pastoral Epistles** Hebrews **Revelation**
Missing books Why is it not in Deuteronomy?	
Added books Why is it in Luke's Gospel?	
What meaning is there in the Old and New Testament You can sit around a table.	
How many verses in the Old Testament Sixty-one.	How many verses in the New Testament Twenty-nine.

1680 BC
Genesis ch.43 v32-33

1280 BC
Exodus ch.25 v29-30; ch.40 v22-23

1240 BC
Numbers ch.3 v31-32

1010 BC
1 Samuel ch.9 v22-23

1000 BC
Psalm ch.128 v3

975 BC
2 Samuel ch.9 v7

950 BC
Proverbs ch.21 v4; ch.25 v7

850 BC
1 Kings ch.2 v7; ch.13 v20-21

570 BC
Ezekiel ch.39 v20

530 BC
Daniel ch.11 v27

445 BC
Malachi ch.1 v12-13

400 BC
Nehemiah ch.5 v17-18

AD 30
Matthew ch.23 v6
Luke ch.14 v7; ch.22 v27, v29-30
John ch.13 v28-29

AD 53
1 Corinthians ch.10 v21-22

AD 55
Romans ch.11 v9

AD 66
Hebrews ch.9 v2-3

Teacher

Most popular Old Testament Ecclesiastes.	Most popular New Testament Luke.
If the book is missing, it would be **bold** **Pentateuch** **Joshua and Judges** History books After captivity **Psalms** Proverbs and Ecclesiastes Major prophets **Minor prophets**	Gospels **Acts** Letters of Paul **Letter of James** **Letters of Peter** Pastoral Epistles **Hebrews** **Revelation**
Missing books Why is it not in the Pentateuch?	
Added books Why is it in Ecclesiastes?	
What meaning is there in the Old and New Testament God is the real teacher.	
How many verses in the Old Testament Fifteen.	How many verses in the New Testament Fifty-four.

1300 BC
Job ch.36 v22

975 BC
1 Chronicles ch.25 v8

950 BC
Ecclesiastes ch.1 v2; ch.12 v9-10

685 BC
Isaiah ch.28 v29; ch.30 v20

450 BC
Ezra ch.7 v12

AD 30
Matthew ch.13 v52; ch.17 v24
Luke ch.11 v45; ch.21 v7
John ch.3 v10

AD 55
Romans ch.12 v7-8

AD 64
2 Timothy ch.1 v11

Thank

Most popular Old Testament	Most popular New Testament
Psalms.	1 Corinthians.

If the book is missing, it would be **bold**	
Pentateuch	Gospels
Joshua and Judges	**Acts**
History books	Letters of Paul
After captivity	**Letter of James**
Psalms	**Letters of Peter**
Proverbs and Ecclesiastes	Pastoral Epistles
Major prophets	**Hebrews**
Minor prophets	**Revelation**

Missing books
Why is it not in Mark's Gospel?

Added books
Why is it in Psalms?

What meaning is there in the Old and New Testament
Most of the thanks will be thanks to God.

How many verses in the Old Testament	How many verses in the New Testament
Twenty-six.	Twenty-five.

1010 BC
1 Samuel ch.1 v18; ch.25 v33-34

1000 BC
Psalm ch.35 v18; ch.79 v13; ch.111 v1; ch.118 v21; ch.119 v7, v62;
ch.138 v4; ch.139 v14; ch.142 v7

975 BC
2 Samuel ch.14 v9
1 Chronicles ch.16 v35; ch.29 v13-14

950 BC
Proverbs ch.30 v11
Ecclesiastes ch.9 v15-16

685 BC
Isaiah ch.43 v20

530 BC
Daniel ch.2 v23

AD 30
Luke ch.10 v21; ch.18 v11
John ch.11 v41

AD 50
2 Thessalonians ch.1 v3-4

AD 53
1 Corinthians ch.10 v30; ch.14 v18-19; ch.15 v57
Philippians ch.4 v6-7

AD 55
Romans ch.7 v25
2 Corinthians ch.2 v14; ch.9 v15

AD 64
2 Timothy ch.1 v3

Theft

Most popular Old Testament Exodus and Amos.	Most popular New Testament Matthew and Mark.
If the book is missing, it would be **bold** Pentateuch **Joshua and Judges** **History books** **After captivity** **Psalms** **Proverbs and Ecclesiastes** **Major prophets** Minor prophets	Gospels **Acts** **Letters of Paul** **Letter of James** **Letters of Peter** **Pastoral Epistles** **Hebrews** **Revelation**
Missing books Why is it not in Proverbs?	
Added books Why is it in Amos?	
What meaning is there in the Old and New Testament A thief is one who takes unlawfully what is not his own.	
How many verses in the Old Testament Two.	How many verses in the New Testament Two.

1280 BC
Exodus ch.22 v3-4

750 BC
Amos ch.3 v10

AD 30
Matthew ch.15 v19
Mark ch.7 v21-23

Thorns

Most popular Old Testament Isaiah.	Most popular New Testament Matthew, Mark, Luke and John.
If the book is missing, it would be **bold** Pentateuch Joshua and Judges History books **After captivity** Psalms Proverbs and Ecclesiastes Major prophets Minor prophets	Gospels **Acts** **Letters of Paul** **Letter of James** **Letters of Peter** **Pastoral Epistles** Hebrews **Revelation**
Missing books Why is it not in Exodus?	
Added books Why is it in Isaiah?	
What meaning is there in the Old and New Testament Thorns can be found in a spiny plant.	
How many verses in the Old Testament Twenty-three.	How many verses in the New Testament Nine.

1680 BC
Genesis ch.3 v18

1240 BC
Numbers ch.33 v55-56

1060 BC
Judges ch.2 v3; ch.8 v16-17

1000 BC
Psalm ch.58 v9

975 BC
2 Samuel ch.23 v6-7

950 BC
Ecclesiastes ch.7 v6

720 BC
Hosea ch.10 v8

690 BC
Micah ch.7 v4

685 BC
Isaiah ch.5 v6; ch.7 v25; ch.9 v18; ch.27 v4-5; ch.55 v13

580 BC
Jeremiah ch.4 v3; ch.12 v13

570 BC
Ezekiel ch.28 v24

AD 30
Mark ch.4 v7
John ch.19 v2-3

AD 66
Hebrews ch.6 v8

Thunder

Most popular Old Testament	Most popular New Testament
Exodus and Job.	Revelation.

If the book is missing, it would be **bold**	
Pentateuch	Gospels
Joshua and Judges	**Acts**
History books	**Letters of Paul**
After captivity	**Letter of James**
Psalms	**Letters of Peter**
Proverbs and Ecclesiastes	**Pastoral Epistles**
Major prophets	**Hebrews**
Minor prophets	Revelation

Missing books
Why is it not in Ezekiel?

Added books
Why is it in Revelation?

What meaning is there in the Old and New Testament
God speaks through the thunder.

How many verses in the Old Testament	How many verses in the New Testament
Twenty-seven.	Nine.

1300 BC
Job ch.26 v14; ch.36 v33 - ch.37 v5

1280 BC
Exodus ch.9 v23; ch.19 v16-17

1010 BC
1 Samuel ch.12 v17

1000 BC
Psalm ch.77 v17-18; ch.104 v7

685 BC
Isaiah ch.17 v12-13

580 BC
Jeremiah ch.10 v13

550 BC
Joel ch.3 v16

AD 30
John ch.12 v29

AD 96
Revelation ch.4 v5; ch.8 v5; ch.16 v18-19; ch.19 v6

Tongue

Most popular Old Testament	Most popular New Testament
Proverbs.	James.
If the book is missing, it would be **bold** **Pentateuch** **Joshua and Judges** History books **After captivity** Psalms Proverbs and Ecclesiastes Major prophets **Minor prophets**	Gospels Acts Letters of Paul Letter of James Letters of Peter **Pastoral Epistles** **Hebrews** **Revelation**
Missing books Why is it not in Matthew's Gospel?	
Added books Why is it in the Letter of James?	
What meaning is there in the Old and New Testament The tongue is a horrible instrument; it is better to keep silent.	
How many verses in the Old Testament Twenty-nine.	How many verses in the New Testament Twelve.

1300 BC
Job ch.27 v4-5

1000 BC
Psalm ch.34 v13; ch.50 v19

975 BC
2 Samuel ch.23 v2

950 BC
Proverbs ch.10 v31; ch.13 v3; ch.18 v21; ch.25 v23

685 BC
Isaiah ch.45 v23

570 BC
Ezekiel ch.3 v26

AD 30
Mark ch.7 v35
Luke ch.16 v24

AD 53
Philippians ch.2 v11

AD 55
Romans ch.14 v11

AD 64
1 Peter ch.3 v10

AD 66
James ch.1 v26; ch.3 v6

Unbelief

Most popular Old Testament	Most popular New Testament
None.	Mark.

If the book is missing, it would be **bold**	
	Gospels
Pentateuch	**Acts**
Joshua and Judges	Letters of Paul
History books	**Letter of James**
After captivity	**Letters of Peter**
Psalms	Pastoral Epistles
Proverbs and Ecclesiastes	Hebrews
Major prophets	**Revelation**
Minor prophets	

Missing books

Why is it not in the Old Testament?

Added books

Why is it in Mark's Gospel?

What meaning is there in the Old and New Testament

We need belief to work with Jesus.

How many verses in the Old Testament	How many verses in the New Testament
None.	Eleven.

AD 30
Matthew ch.13 v58
Mark ch.6 v5-6; ch.9 v24; ch.16 v14

AD 55
Romans ch.11 v23-24

AD 64
1 Timothy ch.1 v13-14

AD 66
Hebrews ch.3 v19

Village

Most popular Old Testament	Most popular New Testament
Genesis.	Luke.

If the book is missing, it would be **bold**	
Pentateuch	Gospels
Joshua and Judges	**Acts**
History books	**Letters of Paul**
After captivity	**Letter of James**
Psalms	**Letters of Peter**
Proverbs and Ecclesiastes	**Pastoral Epistles**
Major prophets	**Hebrews**
Minor prophets	**Revelation**

Missing books
Why is it not in the Letters of Paul, James and Peter?

Added books
Why is it in Genesis?

What meaning is there in the Old and New Testament
A village is a small town closer to the countryside.

How many verses in the Old Testament	How many verses in the New Testament
Sixteen.	Thirty-four.

1680 BC
Genesis ch.19 v20; ch.38 v22

1240 BC
Leviticus ch.25 v31

1060 BC
Judges ch.5 v11

975 BC
2 Samuel ch.16 v5

850 BC
1 Kings ch.17 v10

690 BC
Micah ch.5 v2

580 BC
Jeremiah ch.41 v17-18

AD 30
Matthew ch.21 v2
Mark ch.8 v23
Luke ch.4 v37; ch.7 v12-13; ch.9 v53-54; ch.17 v12-13
John ch.4 v8, v40-42

Vision

Most popular Old Testament	Most popular New Testament
Daniel.	Acts.

If the book is missing, it would be **bold**	
Pentateuch	Gospels
Joshua and Judges	Acts
History books	Letters of Paul
After captivity	**Letter of James**
Psalms	**Letters of Peter**
Proverbs and Ecclesiastes	**Pastoral Epistles**
Major prophets	**Hebrews**
Minor prophets	Revelation

Missing books
Why is it not in Hebrews?

Added books
Why is it in Daniel?

What meaning is there in the Old and New Testament
A vision is where God speaks during the night.

How many verses in the Old Testament	How many verses in the New Testament
Seventy-nine.	Eighteen.

1680 BC
Genesis ch.15 v1; ch.46 v2

1300 BC
Job ch.4 v13

1240 BC
Numbers ch.24 v4

975 BC
2 Samuel ch.7 v17

750 BC
Amos ch.7 v1

685 BC
Isaiah ch.21 v2

630 BC
Nahum ch.1 v1

620 BC
Habakkuk ch.1 v1

580 BC
Jeremiah ch.24 v1
2 Chronicles ch.18 v16

570 BC
Ezekiel ch.3 v23; ch.8 v3
Obadiah ch.1 v1

530 BC
Daniel ch.2 v19; ch.8 v16; ch.10 v7-9

515 BC
Zechariah ch.1 v8

AD 30
Luke ch.1 v22

AD 63
Acts ch.9 v12; ch.11 v5-7; ch.18 v9-10; ch.26 v19-20

AD 50
2 Thessalonians ch.2 v2-3

AD 96
Revelation ch.9 v17

Watch

Most popular Old Testament	Most popular New Testament
Jeremiah.	Mark.

If the book is missing, it would be **bold**	
	Gospels
Pentateuch	Acts
Joshua and Judges	Letters of Paul
History books	**Letter of James**
After captivity	Letters of Peter
Psalms	Pastoral Epistles
Proverbs and Ecclesiastes	Hebrews
Major prophets	Revelation
Minor prophets	

Missing books

Why is it not in the Letter of James?

Added books

Why is it in Jeremiah?

What meaning is there in the Old and New Testament

Watch is to look at something, or to be vigilant.

How many verses in the Old Testament	How many verses in the New Testament
Seventy-seven.	Thirty-five.

1680 BC
Genesis ch.2 v15-16; ch.4 v7

1300 BC
Job ch.36 v18-19

1280 BC
Exodus ch.14 v13-14

1240 BC
Numbers ch.20 v8
Deuteronomy ch.4 v9

1010 BC
1 Samuel ch.2 v32-33

1000 BC
Psalm ch.32 v8; ch.121 v8

975 BC
2 Samuel ch.22 v28

950 BC
Proverbs ch.21 v23
Ecclesiastes ch.5 v11

850 BC
1 Kings ch.9 v3

685 BC
Isaiah ch.6 v9; ch.27 v3

630 BC
Nahum ch.2 v1

620 BC
Habakkuk ch.1 v3

580 BC
2 Chronicles ch.28 v11
Jeremiah ch.24 v6-7

570 BC
Ezekiel ch.40 v4

515 BC
Zechariah ch.12 v4-5

AD 30
Matthew ch.6 v1; ch.24 v42-44; ch.26 v40-41
Mark ch.13 v9
Luke ch.21 v34

AD 54
Galatians ch.5 v15

AD 55
Romans ch.16 v17-18

AD 63
Acts ch.20 v31

AD 64
1 Timothy ch.4 v16
1 Peter ch.3 v12; ch.5 v8-9

AD 66
Hebrews ch.13 v17

AD 93
2 John ch.1 v8-9

Wave

Most popular Old Testament	Most popular New Testament
Judges.	Luke, Acts and James.

If the book is missing, it would be **bold**	
Pentateuch	Gospels
Joshua and Judges	Acts
History books	**Letters of Paul**
After captivity	Letter of James
Psalms	**Letters of Peter**
Proverbs and Ecclesiastes	**Pastoral Epistles**
Major prophets	**Hebrews**
Minor prophets	**Revelation**

Missing books

Why is it not in Matthew's Gospel?

Added books

Why is it in Judges?

What meaning is there in the Old and New Testament

A wave is any movement suggestive of a surge.

How many verses in the Old Testament	How many verses in the New Testament
Nine.	Three.

1060 BC
Judges ch.9 v9

1000 BC
Psalm ch.88 v7

720 BC
Hosea ch.10 v7

685 BC
Isaiah ch.11 v5; ch.13 v2

580 BC
2 Kings ch.5 v11-12

AD 30
Luke ch.8 v37

AD 63
Acts ch.8 v1

AD 66
James ch.1 v6-8

Wealth

Most popular Old Testament	Most popular New Testament
Proverbs.	Luke.
If the book is missing, it would be **bold**	
Pentateuch	Gospels
Joshua and Judges	Acts
History books	Letters of Paul
After captivity	Letter of James
Psalms	**Letters of Peter**
Proverbs and Ecclesiastes	Pastoral Epistles
Major prophets	**Hebrews**
Minor prophets	Revelation
Missing books Why is it not in Hebrews?	
Added books Why is it in Proverbs?	
What meaning is there in the Old and New Testament Man desires wealth.	
How many verses in the Old Testament Ninety-nine.	How many verses in the New Testament Fourteen.

1680 BC
Genesis ch.12 v5; ch.15 v14-15; ch.34 v29

1300 BC
Job ch.15 v29; ch.27 v19

1240 BC
Numbers ch.31 v9-10
Deuteronomy ch.17 v17

1000 BC
Psalm ch.49 v6-7, v20

950 BC
Proverbs ch.3 v9; ch.11 v16; ch.18 v11; ch.23 v5
Ecclesiastes ch.5 v10-11

850 BC
1 Kings ch.3 v11-14

750 BC
Amos ch.3 v10

720 BC
Hosea ch.5 v7

630 BC
Nahum ch.3 v1

580 BC
2 Chronicles ch.32 v29-30
Jeremiah ch.15 v13; ch.48 v7

570 BC
Ezekiel ch.7 v11

530 BC
Daniel ch.11 v2

465 BC
Esther ch.5 v10-11

AD 30
Matthew ch.13 v22
Luke ch.12 v21; ch.16 v11-12

AD 61
Ephesians ch.2 v7

AD 63
Acts ch.19 v25-27

AD 64
1 Timothy ch.6 v6-8

AD 66
James ch.5 v3

AD 96
Revelation ch.18 v19

Weeping

Most popular Old Testament	Most popular New Testament
Jeremiah.	Matthew.

If the book is missing, it would be **bold**	
Pentateuch	Gospels
Joshua and Judges	Acts
History books	Letters of Paul
After captivity	**Letter of James**
Psalms	**Letters of Peter**
Proverbs and Ecclesiastes	**Pastoral Epistles**
Major prophets	**Hebrews**
Minor prophets	Revelation

Missing books
Why is it not in Proverbs?

Added books
Why is it in Matthew's Gospel?

What meaning is there in the Old and New Testament
The Israelites wept aloud; it was customary to do that.

How many verses in the Old Testament	How many verses in the New Testament
Thirty-nine.	Twenty-one.

1680 BC
Genesis ch.45 v14-15

1300 BC
Job ch.17 v7

1240 BC
Numbers ch.14 v1-2

1060 BC
Judges ch.21 v2-3

1000 BC
Psalm ch.6 v6-8

975 BC
2 Samuel ch.13 v36-37

750 BC
Amos ch.8 v10

685 BC
Isaiah ch.65 v19

580 BC
2 Kings ch.8 v11
Jeremiah ch.50 v4

570 BC
Ezekiel ch.7 v27

550 BC
Joel ch.2 v12

450 BC
Ezra ch.3 v13

445 BC
Malachi ch.2 v13-14

400 BC
Nehemiah ch.8 v9

AD 30
Matthew ch.8 v12; ch.26 v75
Mark ch.5 v39; ch.16 v10-11
Luke ch.7 v38; ch.22 v62
John ch.11 v33-36

AD 53
1 Corinthians ch.7 v30

AD 63
Acts ch.9 v39; ch.21 v13

AD 96
Revelation ch.5 v5

Wheat

Most popular Old Testament Exodus and Ezekiel.	Most popular New Testament Matthew.
If the book is missing, it would be **bold** Pentateuch Joshua and Judges History books After captivity Psalms Proverbs and Ecclesiastes Major prophets Minor prophets	Gospels Acts Letters of Paul **Letter of James** **Letters of Peter** **Pastoral Epistles** **Hebrews** Revelation

Missing books Why is it not in Joshua?
Added books Why is it in Ezekiel?
What meaning is there in the Old and New Testament Wheat and barley were the food of the Israelites.

How many verses in the Old Testament Thirty-seven.	How many verses in the New Testament Nineteen.

1300 BC
Job ch.31 v40

1280 BC
Exodus ch.29 v21; ch.34 v22

1240 BC
Deuteronomy ch.8 v8-10

1150 BC
Ruth ch.2 v23

1010 BC
1 Samuel ch.12 v17

1060 BC
Judges ch.6 v11

1000 BC
Psalm ch.81 v16; ch.147 v14

975 BC
2 Samuel ch.4 v6
1 Chronicles ch.21 v23

950 BC
Proverbs ch.20 v26

850 BC
1 Kings ch.5 v11-12

685 BC
Isaiah ch.28 v25

570 BC
Ezekiel ch.27 v17

550 BC
Joel ch.1 v11

AD 30
Matthew ch.3 v12; ch.13 v39
Luke ch.22 v31-32
John ch.12 v24

AD 53
1 Corinthians ch.15 v37-38

AD 96
Revelation ch.18 v13

Wind

Most popular Old Testament	Most popular New Testament
Ecclesiastes and Isaiah.	Acts.

If the book is missing, it would be **bold**	
Pentateuch	Gospels
Joshua and Judges	Acts
History books	Letters of Paul
After captivity	Letter of James
Psalms	Letters of Peter
Proverbs and Ecclesiastes	**Pastoral Epistles**
Major prophets	**Hebrews**
Minor prophets	Revelation

Missing books
Why is it not in Deuteronomy?

Added books
Why is it in Acts?

What meaning is there in the Old and New Testament
The winds are controlled by God.

How many verses in the Old Testament	How many verses in the New Testament
Ninety-five.	Twenty-six.

1680 BC
Genesis ch.8 v1-2; ch.41 v27

1300 BC
Job ch.27 v21-22; ch.37 v17

1280 BC
Exodus ch.10 v19-20; ch.14 v21

1240 BC
Numbers ch.11 v31

1000 BC
Psalm ch.78 v26; ch.148 v8

975 BC
2 Samuel ch.22 v10-11

950 BC
Proverbs ch.25 v23
Ecclesiastes ch.1 v6-7; ch.2 v11

850 BC
1 Kings ch.19 v11-12

750 BC
Jonah ch.1 v4-5; ch.4 v8

720 BC
Hosea ch.4 v19; ch.12 v1

685 BC
Isaiah ch.29 v5; ch.64 v6

620 BC
Habakkuk ch.1 v11

580 BC
Jeremiah ch.4 v11-12; ch.10 v13

570 BC
Ezekiel ch.19 v12

AD 30
Luke ch.8 v25; ch.12 v55-56

AD 61
Ephesians ch.4 v14-15

AD 63
Acts ch.27 v14-15

AD 66
James ch.1 v6-7

AD 80
2 Peter ch.2 v17-18

AD 96
Revelation ch.6 v13-14

Wisdom

Most popular Old Testament	Most popular New Testament
Proverbs.	1 Corinthians.
If the book is missing, it would be **bold** Pentateuch **Joshua and Judges** History books After captivity Psalms Proverbs and Ecclesiastes Major prophets Minor prophets	Gospels Acts Letters of Paul Letter of James Letters of Peter Pastoral Epistles **Hebrews** Revelation

Missing books
Why is it not in John's Gospel?

Added books
Why is it in Proverbs and Ecclesiastes?

What meaning is there in the Old and New Testament
God gives wisdom and understanding.

How many verses in the Old Testament	How many verses in the New Testament
One hundred and Seventy-two.	Fifty-three.

1680 BC
Genesis ch.3 v6

1300 BC
Job ch.11 v6; ch.28 v12-13, v28

1280 BC
Exodus ch.31 v3-5

1240 BC
Deuteronomy ch.4 v6

1000 BC
Psalm ch.111 v10

975 BC
2 Samuel ch.14 v2
1 Chronicles ch.26 v14-15

950 BC
Proverbs ch.2 v6; ch.3 v19; ch.21 v30
Ecclesiastes ch.2 v26; ch.8 v16-17

850 BC
1 Kings ch.3 v10-12; ch.10 v24-25

685 BC
Isaiah ch.11 v2

580 BC
Jeremiah ch.10 v12

570 BC
Ezekiel ch.28 v4-5, v17

530 BC
Daniel ch.1 v17; ch.5 v11

450 BC
Ezra ch.7 v25

AD 30
Matthew ch.11 v19
Luke ch.2 v52; ch.21 v15-17

AD 53
1 Corinthians ch.2 v6-8

AD 55
Romans ch.11 v33

AD 61
Colossians ch.1 v9-10

AD 64
Titus ch.2 v12-13

AD 66
James ch.1 v5-6; ch.3 v17-18

AD 96
Revelation ch.7 v12

Witness

Most popular Old Testament	Most popular New Testament
Proverbs.	Acts and Revelation.

If the book is missing, it would be **bold**	
	Gospels
Pentateuch	Acts
Joshua and Judges	Letters of Paul
History books	**Letter of James**
After captivity	Letters of Peter
Psalms	**Pastoral Epistles**
Proverbs and Ecclesiastes	**Hebrews**
Major prophets	Revelation
Minor prophets	

Missing books

Why is it not in Ezekiel?

Added books

Why is it in Revelation?

What meaning is there in the Old and New Testament

God is our witness. He will make sure that we obey him.

How many verses in the Old Testament	How many verses in the New Testament
Fifty-one.	Twenty.

1680 BC
Genesis ch.31 v49-50

1300 BC
Job ch.16 v19

1280 BC
Exodus ch.23 v1

1240 BC
Numbers ch.35 v30-31
Deuteronomy ch.30 v19

1220 BC
Joshua ch.22 v34

1060 BC
Judges ch.11 v10

1010 BC
1 Samuel ch.6 v18

1000 BC
Psalm ch.50 v4

975 BC
1 Chronicles ch.28 v8

950 BC
Proverbs ch.14 v5

690 BC
Micah ch.6 v1

685 BC
Isaiah ch.30 v8-9

580 BC
Jeremiah ch.42 v5-6

445 BC
Malachi ch.3 v5

AD 30
Matthew ch.26 v60
John ch.5 v36

AD 55
Romans ch.9 v1-2
2 Corinthians ch.1 v23

AD 63
Acts ch.1 v22; ch.26 v16-17

AD 64
1 Peter ch.5 v1

AD 96
Revelation ch.22 v20

Works

Most popular Old Testament Psalms.	Most popular New Testament John's Gospel.
If the book is missing, it would be **bold** Pentateuch **Joshua and Judges** History books **After captivity** Psalms Proverbs and Ecclesiastes Major prophets Minor prophets	Gospels **Acts** Letters of Paul Letter of James **Letters of Peter** Pastoral Epistles Hebrews Revelation
Missing books Why is it not in Genesis?	
Added books Why is it in John's Gospel?	
What meaning is there in the Old and New Testament Good works come from God alone.	
How many verses in the Old Testament Twenty-three.	How many verses in the New Testament Twenty-two.

1300 BC
Job ch.36 v24-25

1280 BC
Exodus ch.31 v14-15

1000 BC
Psalm ch.46 v8; ch.77 v12; ch.92 v5; ch.143 v5

950 BC
Ecclesiastes ch.4 v8

685 BC
Isaiah ch.25 v11; ch.64 v4

620 BC
Habakkuk ch.3 v2

580 BC
2 Chronicles ch.2 v14
Jeremiah ch.51 v17

AD 30
John ch.5 v36; ch.14 v12

AD 53
1 Corinthians ch.12 v6

AD 55
Romans ch.11 v6
2 Corinthians ch.12 v9

AD 61
Colossians ch.1 v29

AD 64
1 Timothy ch.6 v18-19

AD 66
Hebrews ch.10 v24
James ch.2 v26

AD 96
Revelation ch.15 v3

Writing

Most popular Old Testament	Most popular New Testament
Daniel.	1 John.

If the book is missing, it would be **bold**	
Pentateuch	Gospels
Joshua and Judges	**Acts**
History books	Letters of Paul
After captivity	Letter of James
Psalms	Letters of Peter
Proverbs and Ecclesiastes	Pastoral Epistles
Major prophets	**Hebrews**
Minor prophets	Revelation

Missing books

Why is it not in the Psalms?

Added books

Why is it in 1 John?

What meaning is there in the Old and New Testament

People wrote down the words to remember them.

How many verses in the Old Testament	How many verses in the New Testament
Fourteen.	Thirty-eight.

1240 BC
Deuteronomy ch.31 v24-27

975 BC
1 Chronicles ch.28 v19

950 BC
Ecclesiastes ch.12 v12

580 BC
Jeremiah ch.8 v8

530 BC
Daniel ch.5 v12

400 BC
Nehemiah ch.9 v38

AD 30
Luke ch.1 v63

AD 53
1 Corinthians ch.4 v14

AD 54
Galatians ch.1 v20

AD 55
Romans ch.1 v7
2 Corinthians ch.12 v11; ch.13 v10

AD 64
1 Peter ch.5 v12

AD 80
2 Peter ch.1 v1
Jude ch.1 v1

AD 93
1 John ch.1 v4; ch.2 v1, v13, v26

Yoke

Most popular Old Testament	Most popular New Testament
Jeremiah.	Matthew.

If the book is missing, it would be **bold**	
Pentateuch	Gospels
Joshua and Judges	Acts
History books	**Letters of Paul**
After captivity	**Letter of James**
Psalms	**Letters of Peter**
Proverbs and Ecclesiastes	**Pastoral Epistles**
Major prophets	**Hebrews**
Minor prophets	**Revelation**

Missing books

Why is it not in Psalms and Proverbs?

Added books

Why is it in Jeremiah?

What meaning is there in the Old and New Testament

God has the power to yoke his people to enter into slavery.

How many verses in the Old Testament	How many verses in the New Testament
Twenty-seven.	Three.

1240 BC
Leviticus ch.26 v13
Deuteronomy ch.28 v48

720 BC
Hosea ch.10 v11; ch.11 v4

685 BC
Isaiah ch.9 v4

630 BC
Nahum ch.1 v13

580 BC
Jeremiah ch.2 v20; ch.28 v14; ch.31 v18-19
Lamentations ch.3 v27

AD 30
Matthew ch.11 v29-30

AD 63
Acts ch.15 v10-11